PHYSICAL SETTINGS AND ORGANIZATION DEVELOPMENT

FRED I. STEELE
Consultant on Organizational and Environmental Change

ADDISON-WESLEY PUBLISHING COMPANY
Reading, Massachusetts
Menlo Park, California • London • Don Mills, Ontario

This book is in the Addison-Wesley series:

ORGANIZATION DEVELOPMENT

Editors
Edgar Schein
Warren Bennis
Richard Beckhard

 Printed in the United States of America. Published simultaneously in Canada. Library of Congress Catalog Card No. 70-172802.

ISBN 0-201-07211-4
BCDEFGHIJK-CO-79876543

FOREWORD

Since the publication of the original series of six books on organization development (OD), this field has grown rapidly. No longer is it a field in search of a clear self-definition. We now find a large number of books and articles on OD and many competing models of what OD is and should be. All this proliferation of conceptualizing, empirical research, and description of new OD tools is a healthy and welcome development. Apparently, organizations have found that concepts and techniques of organization development are useful and viable, and schools have found that the theory and practice of planned change in organizations is a useful part of their curriculum.

One area of concern that received insufficient attention in the original series was the relationship of the organization to its *environment*. Only the Lawrence and Lorsch volume dealt explicitly with this problem, yet it continues to be one of the most fruitful areas for further exploration. The environment is changing rapidly, and the impact of this change on organizational structure and process must be clearly understood if OD efforts are to remain relevant to organizational realities. The present set of three books takes three quite different perspectives toward this problem in the hope of further stimulating thought and practice.

At the most general level, one can think of the environment as generating a set of values which influence organizational functioning and managerial thought. Roeber has written in a broad vein to describe what some of these value changes have been in the last several decades and how such changes have influenced managerial thinking. At a somewhat more specific level, the environment is a source of information for an organization, and the organization must learn how to process increasingly larger quantities and more complex categories of information. Galbraith addresses this problem by relating how different forms of organization structure have evolved in response to increasingly difficult problems of information processing. Although the analysis of organization structure has always been a difficult problem to deal with systematically, Galbraith has found a way to bring order to this complex area by building on previous theories and integrating them around his information-processing view of organizations.

The environment can also be thought of in more concrete physical terms. Work takes place in a physical environment and is influenced by the nature of that physical environment. Yet virtually no attention is paid to the systematic analysis and manipulation of this portion of the environment. Steele gives us a clear view of some of the issues, provides a diagnostic scheme for the analysis of the environment, and suggests how organizations can set about to create physical environments which are more congruent with organizational goals.

As in our first series, we have not attempted to integrate the work of the different authors. Each gives us his view and his particular perspective on how to use that view to improve organizational functioning. We hope that the reader will be stimulated by these views to better understand his own organization and to begin some new organization development efforts.

March 1973

Edgar H. Schein
Richard Beckhard
Warren G. Bennis

ACKNOWLEDGMENTS

Many people were instrumental in one way or another in providing help to me in the development of the sociophysical approach to organization development. Some were helpful simply through the interesting work they are doing in the area, whereas others provided more direct inputs of challenge, support, and criticism. Although I am grateful to all who have influenced me, I can specifically thank only those who provided the most direct help to me in preparing this book – Edgar Schein, Gary Steele, Chris Argyris, Deborah Jones, and David Sellers.

Boston, Mass.
January 1973

F.I.S.

PROLOGUE

In an old vaudeville joke, a husband returns home unexpectedly in the afternoon, to the discomfort of his wife and her lover. The lover leaps up and hides in the bedroom closet. The husband eventually throws open the door and discovers him. He bellows, "What the hell are you doing in this closet??!!" The lover, standing shivering in his underwear, shrugs and says, "Everybody's got to be someplace."

That is indeed a hard statement with which to argue. We are all someplace all the time, and without even trying. But being there and being aware of the impact that the place is having on us are two different things, and the awareness lags far behind the being.

Since this book is about places, their effect on people and organizations, and how places can be changed, I would like you to do the following simple experiment as a way of orienting yourself to what follows. *Look around you at the place you have chosen to start reading this book. Take several minutes to become fully aware of this place.* What are the features that make it a good place for reading; which features are negative?

Move around for a few minutes to identify several other places where you could be reading this. Why did you choose the place you did? Was it a conscious or unconscious choice?

Think about the things you do to keep from being interrupted by other people while you read. Do you pick an isolated spot or send some kind of signal, such as the direction you face? Would another place nearby make it easier to read? *If so, move to it before you go on to the first chapter.*

CONTENTS

Part 1
AN ORIENTATION

1
BASIC DEFINITIONS

This book is about a new, only half-formed field in the applied behavioral sciences. This field could be called many things: "sociophysical organizational development," "ecological consultation," "environmental organizational change," "settings and organizational change," and so on. Each of these phrases captures only part of the total concept, which strives to use knowledge about behavior and environment/ecology/settings/design as inputs to change activities in human organizations. The focus is on using our understanding of environment and behavior as part of the processes of organizational consultation and change.

PURPOSES OF THE BOOK

Because this book is an effort to help in the development of a new area, it has several purposes. One is to increase the *environmental competence* of both readers and those who are influenced by readers. (I will specify later what I mean by the term environmental competence.) A second purpose is to make readers more aware of an *environmental crisis* in our culture. This is not the crisis of pollution that is of such great national concern today. It is a much more subtle crisis, arising from the fact that people always exist within an environment, and that usually they are in surroundings which are unhelpful or detrimental to what they are trying to do. The crisis here is the lack of fit between needs and settings, and it is much more subtle than poisoned water or air.

Part of this crisis is caused by the fact that needs and preferences change over time – usually faster than the rate of change in our physical settings. This suggests the third purpose of the book: to indicate ways in which *physical environmental changes can be used as a means for starting or supporting social system changes.* Finally, it is my hope that this book will *stimulate further exploration in the field of environment and behavior.* I do not see it as an end in itself, but rather as the beginning of a continuing process of learning from writing, research, and experiences in settings.

These three goals have two additional implications. First, in the desire to reduce our blindness to the impact of physical settings on our lives, many of my examples have been drawn from everyday experiences in work organizations. They are often obvious examples, when taken by themselves, but I believe that their consequences and the patterns which they form are much less obvious. My hope is that readers will reinterpret their own experiences in the light of the model presented here.

Second, this book is different from most of those in the Addison-Wesley Organization Development Series in that my emphasis is more on stimulating awareness than on providing a set of ready-made techniques for change. The sociophysical area does not yet have a full complement of change tools which can be applied in various combinations, although in various chapters I have provided some techniques that I use fairly frequently. In addition, my use of the sociophysical approach to date has been in conjunction with other social system change processes. I do not mean to imply by writing this book that the sociophysical approach is a complete change stratgey in and of itself. Rather, this strategy will be most effective when used in the context of an overall plan for systematic organization development.

ASSUMPTIONS ABOUT READERS

I have assumed that you are engaged in the processes of social system and/or individual change. You may be a consultant on organizational change, a community change consultant, an organization member responsible for facilities decisions, a designer interested in relating your solutions to client needs, or a person who wants to create a more useful, satisfying, or growth-producing relationship between yourself and your surroundings. You may be in more than one of these categories. My assumption for all of these is that you are interested in developing your own and others' ability to deal effectively with the physical world around you.

To provide a practical focus, many of the ideas and processes described here are considered from the standpoint of the professional consultant working to improve the functioning of a human organization. As the paragraph above indicates, however, these ideas are by no means meant to be the exclusive property of consultants. All human activities take place in some kind of setting – everybody must be someplace. Some settings are good for what people are trying to do, some are irrelevant, and many are literally unusable for the purposes for which they were intended. I therefore look upon an understanding of behavior and environment as valuable for consultants, organization members, designers, and people in general – especially in this period of accelerating change in the world.

SOCIAL AND PHYSICAL ORGANIZATION DEVELOPMENT

The roots for this book lie in the field of organization development,[1] a part of the applied behavioral sciences. My own work in sociophysical organization development was stimulated by the observation, repeated many times, that attempts to change an organization's functioning by exclusive attention to social-system properties (formal structure, rules, group norms, interpersonal behavior, power distribution, and the like) were incomplete and did not deal with the full range of factors that influence organizational behavior.

A case example is probably the best way to illustrate what I mean by a lack of support between physical and social factors:

> When several executives in a large organization decided that they wanted to work directly on some of their process problems, they hired a behavioral science consultant to work with them. After a diagnostic period, one of the major issues identified was inappropriate

---

1 See the Addison-Wesley Organization Development Series (1969), especially *Organization Development: Strategies and Models* by Richard Beckhard, and *Organization Development: Its Nature, Origins, and Prospects* by Warren J. Bennis.

> hostility between two units of the organization. To deal with this, an off-site session attended by most members of both groups was held at a conference center. They identified problems, causes, perceptual differences, and possible solutions. They agreed to work on them over time.
>
> When they returned to work, there was some contact across group lines, but it died down fairly soon, and conditions returned to their pre-session state. One reason may have been a lack of resolution of some fundamental areas of mistrust at the off-site session. Another was that the two groups were located on different floors of a high-rise office building, so that they had very little informal contact (probably even less than they needed for the interdependences they had). Over time, the distance separating them resulted in few contacts, and the motivation to continue to get to know and value the other group's members waned in competition with more immediate day-to-day contacts.

This is a simple example of a general principle on which this book is based: if one attempts to make changes in the social functioning of an organization, one must also pay attention to the physical systems which form part of the context for the social system. In the example above, it was one thing to decide that contact between the two groups should increase and quite another to make that happen in the same physical structures that had helped create the social distance in the first place. A systematic organization development process would have included the changes in location or layout that would help increase the familiarity of the groups with one another and decrease distance. As it was, the organization continued to say that it was fitting that the two groups remain distant physically and – by extrapolation – socially.

BASIC DEFINITIONS

There are several terms that need to be defined before we can go further. They are: environment, environmental competence, spaces, and settings.

Environment

I use this term in the most general way, that is, as the total surrounding context for the person or subject of interest. A person's environment is a combination of many forces: physical (temperature, light visible to him, physical objects, other living things); social (norms others hold about how he and others should behave, social structure, messages that are there to be received if he tunes in to them, attempts by others to influence him); economic (means for earning a living, general economic conditions); and so on. Groups and organizations also have environments with a similar variety of forces.

For my purposes in this book, it is useful to think of three successive levels of the environment, each acting as the context for the ones of lesser scale. The largest scale is the *geophysical environment:*[2] the plains, bright light, and winds of western Kansas; the lush vegetation, rolling hills, and warm temperatures of Puerto Rico; or the ocean shore, soot, continuous buildings, and changing seasons of the northeastern United States.

This environment is the backdrop for two others. One is what I call the *technophysical environment*. This is made up of the man-made physical objects in a person's or group's immediate surroundings: furniture, light sources, machines, and the like. Finally, there is the immediate *social environment* within which a person exists: the surrounding people, opinion climate, social norms, and so on.

As shown in Fig. 1.1, a person is surrounded by all three environments; the social environment is surrounded by both the technophysical and geophysical environments; and the technophysical environment is surrounded by the geophysical environment. I have also included in the diagram a fourth "environment," which influences all of the others – the *culture* in which the person is located. By culture I mean the shared history and customs, the accumulated knowledge and common languages, and the totality of "products" of a collection of people over time. Culture influences the norms of the immediate groups in which a person is located; culture affects the development of the technophysical environment through handed-down assumptions about how problems of various types should be solved; and culture alters the natural environment over long periods. In addition, culture invests the geographic environment with symbolic meaning, including those elements of the geophysical environment which should be attended to.[3]

---

2 At this level I include man's largest products – roads, bridges, building complexes, and the like – since they provide a setting that is psychologically related in scale to the natural features of a setting. Man's largest objects become geographic elements influencing the overall climate of a place.

3 Although culture influences all the other environments, it is also influenced by them and, in fact, is often defined by anthropologists as the accumulation of social and technophysical features that have developed in a certain geophysical context.

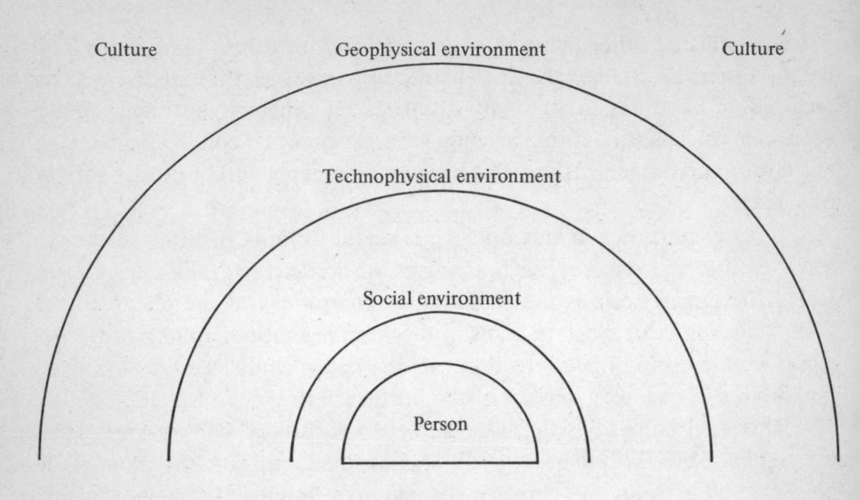

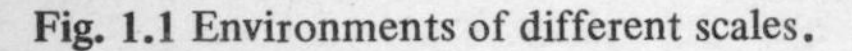

Fig. 1.1 Environments of different scales.

In this book "environment" generally refers to the technophysical setting and occasionally to the geophysical. The "receiver" of environmental influence is the person, group, or organization and the social setting.

Environmental Competence

Two factors constitute environmental competence: (1) the ability to be aware of one's physical environment and its impact; and (2) the ability to use or change that environment to suit one's ends. The thrust here is toward a process which: (a) makes people more aware of the settings around them; (b) inspires them to ask themselves what they are trying to do there; (c) stimulates them to assess the appropriateness of their settings for what they want to experience or accomplish; and (d) leads them to make appropriate changes (in either the setting or their own location, or by leaving it for a better one) to provide a better fit between themselves and the setting.

I believe that as this process is practiced, people become more aware of the impact of their physical surroundings, as well as better able to influence those surroundings in useful ways. These two factors – spatial awareness and skill at developing alternatives and carrying them out – add up to what I am calling environmental competence.

Environmental competence as defined here refers to awareness and use of the *physical* environment. It does not include the degree of skill in dealing with other environments, such as the social setting, economic conditions, or attitudinal climate.

An individual's degree of environmental competence can be determined by his behavior and its outcomes. Similarly, the environmental competence of groups and organizations depends on the degree to which the group is aware of its physical facilities and is able to make good decisions about their use.

Spaces

When used here, this term refers to the places that a particular person, group, or organization usually identifies as home ground. This may or may not be an *exclusive* use – that depends on the situation – but if the members of the group think of these places as available for their activities, then that defines them as part of the group's spaces. Spaces usually have some boundary markers, such as walls, fences, or signs. Thus, the spaces of organizations with their own office buildings are entered when someone walks into the building. If another organization rents the fifth floor of that building, visitors pass through the owner's spaces to get to the tenant's spaces.

Spaces, then, are the territories with which a person, group, or organization is associated. I should also point out that the term "spaces" as used here signifies more than empty locations with geometrical coordinates. I do not mean the empty portions of a volume, but rather the whole volume of a place. Thus, a group's spaces include its offices, meeting areas, traffic routes, and undefined places where people can be. Spaces is therefore simply a convenient term for the places that are potentially available to people, and the term includes more than the voids. Desks, chairs, bulletin boards, and such are a part of a system's spaces, just as the empty floor areas and walkways are.

This definition of spaces also has another dimension: to call the *empty* areas spaces implies that those areas with something filling them at present are not spaces. In fact, space and nonspace are always relative and somewhat arbitrarily liable to change when things such as tables, desks, or partitions are moved to new locations. It therefore helps to think of an organization's total available area as its spaces and to work with it as a potentially filled or free entity.

Settings

The most immediate technophysical surroundings of a person or group as they engage in moment-to-moment existence are their *settings*. Barker (1968) uses the term *behavior setting* to refer to a stable pattern of place and behaviors that therefore represent a psychological milieu for a person when he is present in it. I use settings in a more restricted sense here as the collection of things surrounding a person physically and providing him with immediate sensory stimuli. The setting for an organization can be as large as its immediate physical surroundings: city streets, campus-type lawns, other industrial buildings, and so on. An interior setting, on the other hand, includes the layout of walls and walkways, the things (such as furniture, decorations, machines) in the immediate area, and the people who are in it and around it. For instance, the work setting for a vice-president of a bank in an open-office area includes the visible interior volume of the bank, his desk and chair, the temperature of the air, the light in the room, his fellow employees in the same area, and the customers of the bank who come into it – both those who come into his area and those who walk by him on their way to the tellers' windows. All of these are features that are potentially perceivable by him at a particular time and that therefore make up his setting.

As you can see, a great many things contribute to particular settings. The size of areas people work in is one. The arrangement of those areas is another. Various enclosing structures – walls, partitions, screens, plants – are both things in themselves and things that help to define areas. The kinds of facilities people have – desks, chairs, files, personal artifacts, etc. – fill out the setting. Both the amount and quality of light and noise are both important features, as are the temperature and humidity of the air. Another feature is really a relationship: the relative placement of things to one another, such as a secretary's desk in relation to her boss's or the boss's office in relation to the lavatory.

In a sense, the list above really uses two concepts as if they were one. The first is the actual *things*: structures, air, light, etc. The second is the *properties* of those things: temperature, color, textures, arrangements in different configurations, ease of change, or movement to new locations. In examining the quality or relevance of a setting for the people who use it, we need to question both whether the right things are there and whether they have the appropriate properties that add up to a setting that fits what is needed.

A third level of conceptualization has to do with an implied property of the setting and its things, that is, the *human consequences* of the arrangement and its properties. These include such things as: comfort, visibility of people to one another, moods that a place evokes, memories that it triggers, ease or difficulty of doing various activities there, accidental contacts that occur through movement, and the stimulation of new ideas or feelings.

To summarize, the *environment* refers to the total surroundings for some subject of interest to us, such as a person, a group, or an organization. The subject's *spaces* are those parts of the environment that are identified with him – his territory of operation. Within those spaces are a number of *settings* – the immediate physical surroundings at a particular moment in time. An organization has many settings within its spaces. Settings also exist outside particular, identified spaces; anywhere a person happens to be has features and qualities which make it up, and these form the setting for him at that moment. The extent to which a subject (person or group) makes good use of his settings, spaces, and overall environment is defined as the measure of his *environmental competence.*

AREAS OF THIS BOOK

The next chapter sets the background for sociophysical organization development with a discussion of relevant historical trends. The eight chapters in Part 2 describe a category system which helps us look at the functions that settings play for their users. Six dimensions are described in some detail, and their use in the diagnosis of organizational spatial problems is illustrated in a chapter on the functions in practice.

Part 3 of this book is concerned with environmental competence as a change target. One chapter discusses the causes of environmental incompetence, and a second provides some methods for developing greater competence in both awareness of, and action on, the environment. The final chapter examines a change target of strategic importance – the processes by which decisions about spatial arrangements are made.

2
HISTORICAL CONNECTIONS BETWEEN ORGANIZATION THEORY AND PHYSICAL DESIGN

The purpose of this chapter is to place sociophysical organization development in the perspective of the development of organization and management theory. At first glance the connection may seem rather loose. The fact that there has been so little systematic work in examining the impact of physical settings on management and organizational behavior bears this out. I think this view is misleading, however, and that there are relevant historical trends.

THE HAWTHORNE STUDIES

The Hawthorne studies of Elton Mayo and his associates (Roethlisberger and Dickson, 1939) are generally conceded to mark a turning point in management theory in this country: they were the first to emphasize "human relations" in management and opened the fuzzy world of social and group influences to systematic examination and modification by researchers, writers, and practitioners. The relevance of the Hawthorne experiments to this book is interesting. Those experiments were designed to measure the impact of variations in the physical setting (lighting changes) on the workers' performance (relay assembly and testing of telephone equipment). When the potent influences of group norms and the status satisfaction of being singled out for special treatment were recognized, the original experimental aims of the study were obscured;

that is, they were then seen as being of relatively less importance.

Two reasons for the rather equivocal results of the Hawthorne study of the impact of the physical setting on performance were the simplicity of the variable studied (lighting) and, more important, the expectation that there would be a simple causal link between it and the dependent variable (output). We know enough from environmental research at this point to predict that in most cases the setting acts more as a moderator – a facilitator or inhibitor – of responses which, in turn, combine in complex ways to result in different performance levels.

Another problem was the narrow definition of the independent variable "physical environmental conditions" as lighting and the belief that this was the main environmental manipulation. In fact, the experiments provided two very interesting instances of the impact of physical settings on worker behavior:

a) The observed increase in performance which was attributed to satisfaction with the increased status of being singled out as "special" *was*, in fact, partly a result of the change in the physical environment. The experimental groups were not just *told* that they were to be subjects of an experiment; they were relocated in their own room, away from the rest of the plant. This alteration in setting was a use of spatial language by management to reinforce the message that the workers were now seen as different. In addition, the workers were more often out from under the watching eyes of their supervisors, who had to visit the workroom to see what was happening. Relative locations in an organizational space are as much a part of the physical setting as are more measurable properties such as lighting and temperature.

b) The layout of the rooms allowed easy contact among workers and facilitated the formation and maintenance of group norms concerning behavior and output. Homans (1950) recognized this as a crucial factor in the results that were obtained, noting that the single room increased interaction within the group. He also made a broader point that is relevant here:

> The men were working in a room of a certain shape, with fixtures such as benches oriented in a certain way. They were working on materials with certain tools. These things formed the physical and technical environment in which the human relationships within the room developed, and they made these relationships more likely to develop in some ways than in others. For instance, the sheer

> geographical position of the men within the room had something to do with the organization of work and even with the appearance of cliques.[1]

Later in the book Homans defines what he calls the "external system": those sentiments, interactions, and activities that are developed in a group to deal specifically with survival in the external environment. Other patterns emerge that modify these as the group develops, but it is clear that the environment is reflected in the development of the group. In the Hawthorne experiments, the settings could have been structured so as to promote a pattern of alienation and aloneness rather than one of group cohesion, as evidenced by the existence of a great many fragmented organizations where layouts make real contact impossible.

It is not surprising that the really important impact of the physical setting on the social system results of the Hawthorne studies has not been followed up or had much impact on the theory of management. Most people in our culture tend to be blind to the impact of the physical environment on their day-to-day lives, especially their work lives. It is with good reason that E.T. Hall (1966) titled his book on the use of space *The Hidden Dimension.*

During a number of years of acting as consultant to different kinds of organizations, I have consistently found that most organizations, as well as individuals, are blind to environmental impacts. Organizational policies pay less attention to the impact of physical settings on behavior than to the impact of the "task" environment – the nature of the work world in which members strive toward their chosen organizational goals. It follows that organizations are also usually a good deal less competent at dealing with spatial decision-making than they are in dealing with decisions related to their product, service, markets, and so on. Like many individuals, organizations tend to be deficient in what I referred to in Chapter 1 as basic environmental competence.

SEARCHES FOR "THE" ANSWER

Although in the years since the Hawthorne experiments little attention has been paid in management theory to the physical setting, there have been some efforts in this area. From time to time fads develop and go the

---

1 G. Homans, *The Human Group*. New York: Harcourt Brace & World, 1950, pp. 88-89. Reprinted by permission.

rounds of different organizations. In one period, the private cubicle was "in"; in another the "bull pen" was the answer to the puzzling office layout problem; and most recently the "office landscape" system has been hailed by some as "the" solution. These and many other developments (Muzak, the clean desk theory, etc.) have one feature in common; they all tend to be fed by management's wish for a single "right" solution to the arrangement of the setting in an organization. As such, they were all fairly equally doomed to be disappointing in practice, since they were based on current popularity or on the desire to find an easy mechanism for manipulating subordinates rather than on an analysis of the present and changing needs of a particular group engaged in particular tasks. One of the themes I wish to stress here is that *any universal solution applied to all settings is likely to be inappropriate at least as often as it is appropriate.* Settings must vary with the particular people and activities for which they are used.

THE SOCIOTECHNICAL APPROACH

An effort to match design with specific activities is the *sociotechnical systems* approach (Trist *et al.*, 1963); research based on this approach and applied to various kinds of work systems is still going on. The fundamental concept is that any complex system functions as a result of the interlocking influences of its social, physical, and technological structures. In a classic study, Trist and Bamforth (1951) demonstrated that a new form of technology and task structure had a major impact on the social structure of coal mine work groups and hence on the workers' satisfaction. However, the sociotechnical approach has focused mostly on task and related machine structures (which often have implications for spatial features) rather than on the interrelation of social systems with spatial system features.

PLANT LOCATION

One area of specialized service has touched upon a part of what I consider to be sociophysical organizational design, namely, plant and office location. Today, there are many firms that now provide location analysis as a service to organizations contemplating a move. These specialists consider a range of factors such as costs, ease of performing basic tasks, availability of personnel, and congruence between location and the organization's identity. When done well, a location study can enhance an organization's ability to use its setting well, although all too often the structuring of the interior spaces undoes much of what is accomplished by a good choice of location. Casual observation also suggests that in many instances locational decisions are in the end made primarily on cost grounds alone, with sociophysical considerations (such as whether the location is congruent with the organization's sense of its mission) carrying little weight.[2]

LAYOUT AND EFFICIENCY

Another trend has been the growth of a practitioner- (rather than research-) oriented group – the "efficiency experts" that were in prominent view in the 1940s and 1950s. They are less visible but probably more numerous today, as organizations strive to make ever more rational decisions about the use of their resources. As a part of their analyses, these experts sometimes recommend changes in physical relationships in order to facilitate rapid exchange of paper or verbal instructions, but their primary focus keeps them from going much beyond this simplistic model of the impact of space on systems. They tend to use only readily quantifiable factors, such as time or mistakes, as dependent variables, and so also tend to pass over many of the more subtle effects of settings, such as those on mood or social contacts. For example, a work station may be reorganized in a way that is theoretically very efficient, but less work will actually be done if the user hates being there and seizes every opportunity to leave the station.

A more up-to-date and more sophisticated spatially oriented efficiency approach is that of the office landscape (*Burolandschaft*) exponents from Germany (*Progressive Architecture,* 1968; Kurtz, 1969). The aim of this approach is specifically work-flow oriented: to design a layout that fits the actual work "happenings" in a system and to facilitate these through appropriate spatial arrangements. The proponents of this approach have also very intentionally moved away from the notion that layouts need to be rectilinear. Instead, they design "landscapes" with paths and areas after extensive studies of the flows and contacts of the

2 This is an example of the "inconspicuous costs" phenomenon (in this case, the costs of bad choices) to system functioning discussed in the last chapter of this book.

system at work. Figure 2.1 shows a diagram of an office landscape layout with a grid superimposed to show the contrast between old, right-angled desk arrangements and the more flowing layout of the "landscape" with its curving paths and clumps of desks.

For our purposes, this approach is interesting, but it goes only part way toward a model. The main difference between it and what this book represents is that its practitioners tend to create a form that mirrors what the organization *is*, whereas consultants using sociophysical notions are working to bring the system to what it should and potentially *can be*, with physical changes being facilitators of this development. The office landscape approach, by comparison, is relatively more static.

SPACE PLANNERS

The office landscaping movement is actually one piece of a more general field that has developed over the last ten years or so – the field of space planning. There are now a fair number of space-planning firms that provide comprehensive planning and design services to clients, usually business organizations.[3]

Space-planning firms have skills in economic analysis, interior design, and engineering. Such firms clearly can help an organization avoid major mistakes in planning for future space needs. Once again, however, space-planning firms tend to be less sophisticated in the areas of organizational behavior and organization development. They often work more comfortably in terms of square footage and head counts than in terms of the spatial language of a particular organization and what that language may require or suggest about future space needs. They are even less equipped to bring about spatial changes which actually require fundamental changes in power structure or social system values in order to be effective.

There is a clear role to be played by a behaviorally oriented organization consultant working *in collaboration with* space planners. I want to be clear that in writing this book I am not suggesting that organizational consultants become amateur designers or that designers become amateur psychologists. I am suggesting that each group can go a

---

3 For recent descriptions of work in this profession, see Kurtz (1969) and Mogulescu (1970).

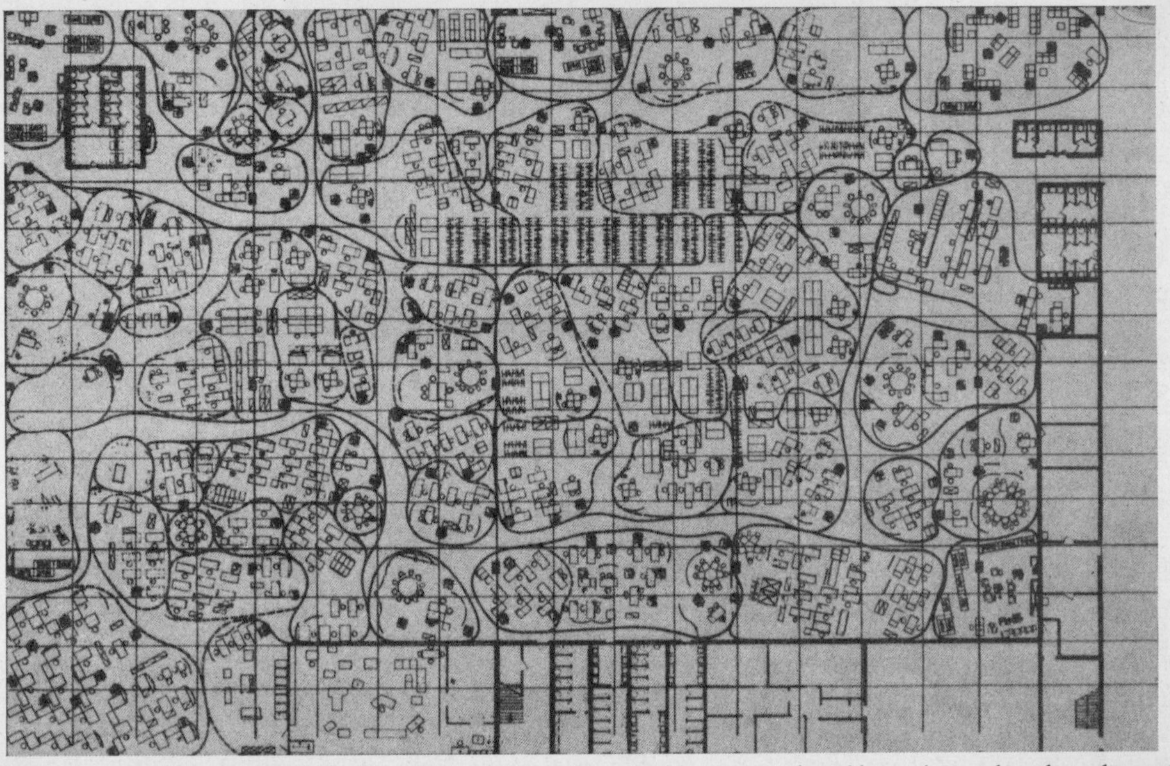

Fig. 2.1 A diagram of a typical Quickborner Office Landscape layout, with a rectangular grid superimposed to show the contrast to the typical regularity of most office layouts. (Reprinted from *Progressive Architecture*.)

lot further toward being aware of the efforts of the other and by pooling resources with the other to promote systematic organizational growth.

STATUS SYMBOLS

The last trend I will discuss here is an area where there *has* been a relatively high awareness of the physical setting in organizations – the area of status symbols. The process is one in which a person's position in the hierarchy is represented symbolically by the nature and layout of the facilities identified with him. Each organization has its own language and set of symbols such that insiders (and knowledgeable outsiders) can tell where a person fits by looking at his personal setting. The symbols used are similar in many systems, however. Mogulescu (1970) provides an example on office size:

> Each individual requiring private office space was assigned to an A+, A, B, C, or D category, depending on his echelon and personal functional needs. Of course, other distinctions in echelon or work function can be made by the assignment of furnishings and equipment to these offices. . .[4]

Carpets are another almost universal symbol, as indicated by the advertisement, "A title on the door rates a Bigelow on the floor." Keys to the executive washroom were immortalized forever in the stage musical *How to Succeed in Business Without Really Trying.*

Status symbols will be discussed in more detail in the section on symbolic identification as a function of settings. I mention them in this review of historical trends because they are the most frequently recognized instance of organizational physical design. In fact, one colleague asked me why I would bother to discuss them at all, since they were "old hat." I agree with him that they are well discussed, but *not* that they are well understood. It is not often recognized that organization status is only one kind of symbolic identification for which settings are used. Many other messages, such as personal preferences, interpersonal desires, aspirations, and the like, are sent by peoples' use of space.

---

4 Reprinted by permission of the publisher from *Profit Through Design.* © 1970 by the American Management Association, Inc.

Bets are now open on whether "echelon" or "personal functional needs" carried more weight in the decisions.

In addition, status symbols are met with various reactions ranging from reverence to ridicule, depending on how a person feels about them, but there has been little examination of the *costs* to an organization of using this particular means for identification. A great deal of time and energy goes into decisions about status symbols. What do organizations give up in the way of flexibility, adaptive use of facilities, and motivation in those who are told symbolically that they are not very important? This question will be examined later; the point here is that few organizations consciously examine the gains and costs of their particular system of status symbols.

It seems to me that the time is overripe for a reconnection with the circle that began with the Hawthorne studies' notions about environmental impact. In the last five years there has been a great upsurge of research on environmental design and its impact on human behavior. As yet, however, this research has had relatively little impact on the actual design or alteration of organizational settings. Neither organizational development consultants nor designers have applied more complex views of man in his environment to live organizations. I hope that this book will provide a useful frame of reference for readers to develop these more complex views.

Part 2
THE FUNCTIONS OF PHYSICAL SETTINGS

3
AN INTRODUCTION TO THE FUNCTIONS OF SETTINGS

There are six basic dimensions that represent the various functions of physical settings. The next six chapters will describe these dimensions with examples, followed by a chapter on the use of the dimensions as an aid to organizational consultation.

The first purpose of this breakdown into dimensions is to help sort out the various functions that settings play for people, in order to answer questions such as: Is this a quality environment for these people? If not, what alterations would improve it? What do they really want from their spaces? and so on. The second purpose is to overcome a general tendency in organizational literature to treat the physical setting in terms akin to Herzberg's notion of a "hygiene" factor, that is, one that acts only as a potential damper on worker morale. As these functional dimensions will illustrate, I believe that the impact of physical settings on organizational life is much more complex than simply as an agent contributing to or reducing morale.

THE NATURE OF "FUNCTIONALITY"

In the field of architecture a dictum was developed in this century to counterbalance the influence of the Beaux Arts, or decorative, tradition in design. The dictum was "Form follows function," and concerned architects hoped that this stance would lead to an architecture and interior design oriented less toward sculpture for its own sake and more toward serving the needs of the people who use it. I believe that this attempt, unfortunately, has not resulted in a more user-oriented architecture.

There are two reasons why the attempt has failed. First, there usually is no elegant, "one best solution" to a particular functional need; thus, an analysis of the functions of a particular structure does not provide designers with "the" right design.

The second, even more limiting, reason is more relevant to the main theme of this book, i.e., designers and users have both had a relatively meager understanding of the functions that settings play for people and a very limited vocabulary for analyzing and discussing these functions in ways that could lead to design criteria. Not only has there been little awareness of man's relationships to his settings, but there has been little recognition that the form-follows-function guide is inadequate if *several* functions are provided by a given structure. The dilemma is that the design implications of these functions often conflict with one another. If one does not recognize different functions of space, it is obviously very difficult to balance out conflicts among these different functions.

For a recent example, we can take the "Offices of the Year" awards given by a magazine in the field of administrative management. The First Award winner was described as "a place for people as well as for working." In addition:

> But on the human side, detailed surveys were made of individual storage and space needs, special working requirements, and the like. It was found, for instance, that 7 X 4 X 1/2 feet is the space needed to comfortably hang a man's coat. Free-standing 7-ft high wardrobe units now conveniently separate work and heavy traffic areas . . .[1]

Leaving aside the fascinating question of whether your coat or mine would be truly comfortable in a 7 X 4 X 1/2 foot space, this example illustrates a not unusual situation – a very simplistic view of human needs in relation to physical settings. My own observations have convinced me that many of the important transactions between person and environment go unrecognized in most organizations. Only relatively trivial or simplistic ones are noticed and dealt with.

---

1 Reprinted from "Offices of the Year," *Administrative Management*, 31, 3, 1970, p. 39. © Geyer-McAllister Publications, Inc.

THE DIMENSIONS

In order to overcome this state of affairs, I developed a system for categorizing the functions that immediate physical settings play for people. My aim was to define categories specific enough to capture major pieces of man's experience in the physical environment, yet broad enough to result in a manageable number of categories. These are the dimensions:[2]

1. *Security and Shelter* refer to protection from harmful or unwanted stimuli in one's surroundings, such as a roof keeping out the rain or a thick wall keeping sounds out of the bedroom.

2. *Social Contact* refers to the arrangements of facilities and spaces that permit or promote social interaction, such as a garden apartment's central bank of mailboxes where people accidentally come face-to-face with one another.

3. *Symbolic Identification* refers to the messages sent by settings which tell someone what a person, group, or organization is like, such as the things a person exhibits in his office.

4. *Task Instrumentality* refers to the facilities and layouts appropriate for carrying out tasks in a particular setting, such as a sound-proof room for taping records.

5. *Pleasure* refers to the pleasure or gratification the place gives to those who use it, such as the views hikers enjoy while visiting the Olympic Peninsula in Washington.

6. *Growth* refers to the stimulus for growth the setting gives the user, such as when a person learns something new about himself from his feelings while lost in a dark woods overnight.

Each of these dimensions will be discussed in some detail. Since the major focus of this book is sociophysical organization development, a large percentage of the examples will be from group and organizational life, especially life in work organizations.

Although I will not present a long derivation here, I should note that these categories were inspired by two main sources: Maslow's (1954) theory of basic human needs, and my own and others' observations of the activities in which people engage in different settings, including their complaints about the inadequacies of the settings for their needs.

4
FUNCTION I: SHELTER AND SECURITY

The most fundamental function of man's immediate physical surroundings is to provide shelter and security from unpredictable, undesirable, or destructive variations in his surroundings. This protection corresponds to Maslow's notion about the most basic level of human needs – the physiological and safety needs. One can be protected from physical elements of a particular geophysical location (cold, rain, wind, bugs, etc.) or from sociopsychological elements (noise, crowds, and the prying eyes of people who may be a threat).

PHYSICAL SHELTER

First, let us consider the physical aspects of shelter. Large numbers of people in the world live in settings that lack adequate protection, heat, light, and mechanical facilities. In our own country many people are voicing grave concern about the large amount of substandard housing. However, since work organizations form the main context here, I will not discuss the issue of adequate shelter for living. (I do recommend, however, that those who are interested in this subject read Orwell's (1937) descriptions of the miners' houses he visited at Wigan Pier.)

The provision of physical security in organizations is clearly related to the whole setting in which work takes place. Orwell provides a fine example of a negative-shelter setting from his experience working in the kitchens of a Paris hotel:

> Our cafeteria was a murky cellar measuring twenty feet by seven by eight high, and so crowded with coffee-urns, breadcutters and the like that one could hardly move without banging against something. It was lighted by one dim electric bulb, and four or five gas-fires that sent out a fierce red breath. There was a thermometer there, and the temperature never fell below 110 degrees Fahrenheit – it neared 130 at some times of the day. At one end were five service lifts, and at the other an ice cupboard where we stored milk and butter. When you went into the ice cupboard you dropped a hundred degrees of temperature at a single step; it used to remind me of the hymn about Greenland's icy mountains and India's coral strand.[1]

Similarly stressful settings exist in many kinds of industries: mining, food processing, many kinds of manufacturing, and winter construction work, to name a few. The stresses are bad weather, noise, extremes of temperature, noxious smells, and cramped quarters. The development of health and safety standards in this country has corresponded to an interest in restructuring settings to make them physically more tolerable.

Today, the physiological stresses of work settings for white collar, professional, and managerial workers tend to be relatively controlled, because the new technologies allow for tight building systems, good artificial light sources, and automatic control of temperature and humidity. Employees have become so adapted to these new levels of comfort, however, that they notice and are disturbed when the controls break down.

I shall discuss later the fact that psychological security needs are a function of the individual's personality and preference. The point here is that an adequate setting for physiological sheltering depends on both the survival range for human beings in general *and* the levels to which the individual has become adapted. For example, I recently observed a steel band from the Bahamas playing indoors in Montreal with coats, hats, and gloves on; I was in my shirtsleeves at the time.

From *Down and Out in Paris and London*, pp. 45-46. New York: Harcourt, Brace and Jovanovich, copyright 1933 by George Orwell. Copyright renewed 1960 by Sonia Pitt-Rivers. Reprinted by permission of Brandt & Brandt.

In keeping with Maslow's notion that physiological and safety needs are prepotent, i.e., must be satisfied to some degree before higher-order needs such as task accomplishment come into play, I see shelter and security as a function which, if not fulfilled by the setting, makes it difficult for the other functions to be met. For instance, Caplan and Lindsay (1946) found that the output of coal miners fell off in a warm, humid environment and that the greatest decrement was toward the end of the shift, when fatigue was added to the physical environmental stress.

A more personal example is my own experience with writing. It is very difficult for me to concentrate and produce if I am in a cold or extremely noisy setting. Another author once indicated that he was sure that the myth of the struggling writer, creating in the icy garret, was just that, a myth. He said that such writers may have attained some juicy life experiences for material while suffering, but that they damn well didn't do much writing while they were in physically uncomfortable surroundings. Apparently his mind, like mine, tends to dwell at such times on dreams of comfort rather than on dreams of genius.

Settings provide physical safety from more than just the natural elements. Structures are also more or less effective at protecting men from others who would harm them. Throughout history, some cities have been defendable against attack due to their location, the way in which the walls were constructed, etc., and others have not. Similarly, forts played an important role in America's history.

In America today the closest analogy to the fort is the fenced enclave that is being built as a "secure" living area for citizens who fear for their property or their lives. The *Boston Globe* recently described a new apartment tower complex being built on the waterfront. It will have only one entrance and an armed guard. Similarly, there is a new design lore in universities about the problem of making administration and records areas "demonstrator-proof." Businesses, also, are now giving considerable attention to ways of protecting their property and employees from intrusion or destruction by dissident elements in the society. The same design problem exists for American embassies throughout the world especially in countries with a history of using the embassy building as a symbolic scapegoat on which to take out hostility toward America.

Our most conspicuous enclave in this country is probably the White House, where the President's home is literally his castle. In his newspaper column, Buckley (1970) described a recent visit: "We arrived in a piercing cold wind at one of those little gates in which three or four uniformed guards sit surrounded by devices devoted to protecting the inmates of the White House against unwanted visitors." Buckley gave this example to illustrate the kind of thing that gives a citizen the feeling "that the Administration is cold and soulless." I had a similar experience and was struck by how much the security function overshadows all others in the White House area. The White House is, in a sense, a monument to the lack of trust in the American people's ability to control their aggressive impulses. This message is even clearer when we compare the White House with the home of another government head, the Prime Minister of England. The doorway of 10 Downing Street can be passed by anyone, and the only sign of imposed social distance is a policeman standing discreetly to the side of the door.

PSYCHIC SECURITY

The second side of the security function is just as, or even more, important to man's existence as is simple physical protection. The setting should provide *psychic security* to its users, i.e., a sense of not being overwhelmed by one's surroundings. Many studies have shown that overstimulation without some control of number and kinds of stimuli can have a deteriorating effect on both humans and animals (Hall, 1966). In particular, overcrowding, and its accompanying bombardment of sights, touches, sounds, and smells tends to disrupt important social functions and control mechanisms and, therefore, be psychologically threatening. In addition, if people cannot get away from others when their aggressive impulses are high, they are more likely to act these impulses out. Social contacts cannot be made privately, but rather must always occur under the scrutiny of third parties, leading to the stressful feeling of always performing for an audience.

Overcrowding is a phenomenon that can occur easily in a work organization that makes space layout calculations based on purely mechanistic notions of the amount of space taken up by bodies and movement. Crowding is in large part a psychological and social phenomenon, not an engineering measure. Whether a layout *seems* crowded will depend on the norms and needs of the people who use it. For instance, it has been found in Canadian university dormitories that room densities preferred by French-speaking students seem too crowded to English-speaking students. The norms of the two groups differ as to how much contact is appropriate and how physically close that contact should be.[2]

Groups, as well as individuals, can suffer if they are not obtaining sufficient shelter in their settings. The climate during the meetings of one staff group I observed was very antagonistic. This changed fairly rapidly after they moved to another room in their building. The original room had been on the sixth floor of a building on a very busy street corner. The group members had been unaware of the energy and strain required to hold discussions while street noises bombarded them, and this strain had been taking its toll. The new room in the interior of the building was a much more protective setting, and in it the climate of the group was more friendly and relaxed.

Goffman (1959) describes another way in which physical settings provide psychic shelter for their users, especially for groups that are organized for some purpose. He suggests that social systems maintain stability and that members carry out their "performances" by having settings that are separated into "front-stage" areas where contact with the public takes place (e.g., a restaurant dining room) and "back-stage" areas that are generally reserved for insiders only (such as the kitchen or scullery). These latter areas provide a setting where role performers can from time to time step out of their assigned social roles, let their hair down, play, and reduce tension. When the setting is structured so that it is difficult to separate front- and back-stage areas (if customers must pass through the kitchen to get to the lavatories), the protective function is unreliable, and tensions are higher.

The word that probably best catches the flavor of the psychological security issue in organizational settings is *privacy*. When people complain of not having enough privacy, they are usually saying that they have no way of *controlling* their relation to their social surroundings because: (a) they cannot control who comes into contact with them and when; (b) they cannot prevent their conversations from being overheard; or (c) they cannot prevent being observed by others. Privacy is therefore a result of having *control* over the amount and quality of the visual and auditory cues sent and received.

---

2 This suggests that it is also possible to have a setting that has high psychic stress through *too little* contact. I will discuss this aspect more fully in the section on social contact as a spatial function.

The "party wall" in apartment buildings is a good example of a structural feature that provides visual privacy but often fails on both the sending and receiving aspects of auditory privacy. Raven (1967) reports that people who complained about lack of privacy in their apartment meant both that they could hear the adjoining family *and* that their own behavior was constrained to nonnoise-producing activities because they, too, could be heard by the neighbors. A similar effect in office settings, has been reported to me many times.

To determine the appropriate amount of privacy for different people or groups, one must understand the user's style, his needs, and what he is trying to do. For instance, one company executive decided that it would be a "good" thing if all members of one department sat out in the open in a "bullpen" so that they could see each other. He soon received visible feedback that this violated some needs for privacy. Purchases of filing cabinets shot up, although storage requirements had not changed. Since "walls" as such were not allowed, people were requisitioning filing cabinets to screen themselves from the constant view of others. In another firm that decided on open offices, the private conference rooms were immediately scheduled for more than a year in advance.

Hall (1966) described in nice detail the way needs for privacy vary with cultural origin. He points out, for instance, that childhood experiences condition the middle- and upper-class Englishman not to expect a room of his own, that is, not to have privacy built into the physical setting. Americans of the same social development expect just the opposite. "As a consequence, the English are puzzled by the American need for a secure place in which to work, an office." Hall also suggests that this results in different strategies for *getting the privacy desired*:

> When the American wants to be alone he goes into a room and shuts the door – he depends on architectural features for screening . . . The English, on the other hand, lacking rooms of their own since childhood, never developed the practice of using space as a refuge from others. They have in effect internalized a set of barriers [not looking at the other person, moving away, etc.], which they erect and which others are supposed to recognize.[3]

---

3 E. Hall, *The Hidden Dimension,* Garden City: Doubleday, 1966, p. 131. Reprinted by permission.

There are two points to the notion of cultural differences in the definition and means of obtaining privacy. One is that international companies must be aware of differing cultural norms among their various employee groups. They should not expect standard behavior from standard settings, as if company policy could wipe out those differences. The second is that even within a national culture, organizations develop their own cultures based on their members' needs, the tasks being done, and the climate of the social system. A publishing firm, for example, will develop a set of norms about privacy different from those of a shoe manufacturing plant.

What happens when the setting does not provide control of contacts? People at work may flee from a setting which they feel is unbearably intrusive, as this manager often did:

> They recently moved another man into the room which had been my office alone. He often wants to talk, and also other people seem to be passing by and stopping in a lot. When I want to really get something done, I sneak up to a penthouse conference room that nobody knows about. It is comfortable, quiet, and has a blackboard. I can do a lot there, and almost nothing in my office.

For many organization members, however, the hidden room is not an alternative. They have an area to which they are assigned, and their performance is judged in part on simple presence in that area. If they often feel intruded upon there, they do not have the choice of leaving or restructuring the area, so they have to live with the bad situation. Over time, the costs of this locked-in feeling may be considerable in terms of both reduced efficiency and psychic energy used to push down uncomfortable feelings of being intruded upon.

Finally, the potency of space as a satisfier or dissatisfier of the dimension of privacy was best brought home to me by a plant manager I observed. After listening patiently to a sales talk from his boss on the wonderful advantages of an open-office layout where everyone would be visible to everyone else, he summed up his personal reaction: "I don't care how great it is. I still say, if I can't fart in it, it's not an office!"

5
FUNCTION II: SOCIAL CONTACT

This dimension deals with the extent to which physical settings facilitate or inhibit interpersonal contact. Although it is true that the quality of interaction has a major influence on security, task performance, pleasure, and growth, the emphasis of this function is on social contact as an end in itself.

To observe this dimension, you really have to look at two aspects: first, the impact of the setting on the amount and quality of the social contacts it provides; and second, the kinds of contacts the users *want* and whether there is a good fit between their wishes and the actual impact of the setting. In explaining these aspects, I will look at three properties of the setting: arrangements of facilities, locations of people in relation to one another and to activities, and the amount of mobility allowed by a setting.

INFLUENCE OF FACILITIES ARRANGEMENTS

There are several kinds of impact that spatial arrangements have on the amount of interpersonal interaction. One influence, first identified by Humphrey Osmond, is the "sociopetal" and "sociofugal" aspect of settings. These are, respectively, the tendency of arrangements to bring people together (as in the small waiting room of a doctor's office, or sitting around a small card table), or to push them apart (as in airport waiting rooms, or large living rooms where furniture is far apart). Sommer (1969) provides a very moving description of the mental hospital setting in which sociofugal space had been so graphically and proudly designed as an "improvement."

> Most of the chairs on this ward stood in straight lines along the walls, but there were several rows back-to-back in the center; around several columns there were four chairs, each chair facing a different direction! . . . With as many as 50 ladies in the large room, there were rarely more than one or two brief conversations. The ladies sat side by side against the newly painted walls in their new chrome chairs and exercised their options of gazing down at the newly tiled floor or looking up at the new florescent lights . . . The arrangement of furniture is left to the ward staff who do not realize the therapeutic potential for furniture arrangement. Ward geography is taken for granted, and a chair becomes something to sweep around rather than a necessary tool for social interaction.[1]

Imagine yourself trying to *maintain* your sanity in that kind of setting, let alone trying to improve from an already shaky position!

I should add that there is another factor which allows this arrangement to be distancing. Not only mental patients, but most of us, tend to take our spatial arrangements as we find them. Unless the furniture is actually bolted down (as is, unfortunately, often the case, especially in universities), a given arrangement can remain sociofugal only if people assume it is fixed. This is an example of what I call "pseudo-fixed feature space" (PFF) – settings that are treated as fixed, even though they are changeable. Pseudo-fixed feature space will be discussed in detail in Chapter 11.

In a series of experiments with seating arrangements, Sommer (1967b) found that an across-corner arrangement was preferred for seated conversations, with across-the-table arrangements being second, and side-by-side arrangements preferred least. Settings that allow only side-by-side

---

1 R. Sommer, *Personal Space: The Behavioral Basis of Design*, pp. 78-79. © 1969. By permission of Prentice-Hall, Inc.

seating, such as many classrooms or terminal waiting rooms, tend to reduce contact, particularly between people who are not in adjacent seats.

This last point raises the issue of fixed versus variable seating arrangements. In classrooms with fixed seats, individual students have difficulty relating to anyone but the teacher at the front or the students on either side, and even they are often too close for comfortable conversation. On the other hand, movable furniture, when combined with group norms which support changing the arrangements when appropriate, can facilitate different amounts of interaction, as desired.

A recent example of this structural flexibility is a living room designed for my Prickley Mountain, Vermont, house by Thomas Luckey (see Fig. 5.1). The room has *no* furniture but is *all* furniture, since any part of the room can be sat on, walked on, etc. People can arrange themselves in many different patterns. My use of this space for different social activities has confirmed that interaction is facilitated by wide choice about how to arrange oneself. Conversely, it is also easy to find a fairly private spot when that seems appropriate.

The arrangement of furniture in offices is an obvious area where the ideas above need to be applied. Spaces can be arranged to keep people apart or bring them together, depending on where chairs, sofas, desks, etc., are placed. Occupants of offices often use their "props" to regulate the distance between themselves and others. Hall (1966) summarizes the impact of this effect:

> Business and social discourse conducted at the far end of social distance (seven to twelve feet) has a more formal character than if it occurs inside the close phase (four to seven feet). Desks in the offices of important people are large enough to hold visitors at the far phase of social distance. Even in an office with standard-sized desks, the chair opposite is eight or nine feet away from the man at the desk. At the far phase of social distance, the finest details of the face, such as the capillaries of the eye, are lost.[2]

As the paragraph above suggests, arrangements affect not only the quantity but also the quality of social contact. Steinzor (1950) noted that when a man in a discussion group finished speaking, the next speaker was often someone *across* from him rather than *next* to him. From this,

---

2 E. Hall, *op. cit.*, p. 115. Reprinted by permission.

Fig. 5.1 A room for flexible social groupings. (From *Glamour*; © 1969 by The Conde Nast Publications Inc.)

Steinzor formulated the "expressive contact hypothesis," namely, that since visual contact is easier with those who can be seen without turning or without violating social distance norms, people are more likely to be aware of, and therefore responsive to, those across from them.

In the office situation, the implication is that in both group sessions and individual work activities in a common area, people will tend to be more aware of others whom they can see easily than those whom they cannot see. Physical arrangements obviously play a major role in visual contacts. We must also note, however, that the social setting also affects this contact process. Hearn (1957) found that the type of leadership in a group affected the responsiveness pattern. With minimal leadership, Steinzor's effect was duplicated. But with a strong leader present, responses tended to come from adjacent people. This is a good example of the joint influence of the physical and social environments.

The Steinzor effect also illustrates that the arrangement of facilities affects more than just the *amount* of contact that people can have. It also affects the *quality* of those contacts. Although we tend to talk about contact as simply present or absent, the fact is that there are different kinds of contact: temporary, constant, surface, intimate, playful, work-oriented, open, closed, and so on.

For example, although there are no hard data, preliminary interviews indicate that one outcome of the open-office landscape plan is that while general interaction of a group tends to increase through greater visibility and ease of movement, social contacts of a more intimate nature tend to decrease. As people feel more doubts about the privacy of their conversations, both visually and verbally, they tend to make the conversations less personal, though more frequent.

Of course, we would expect this influence to be mediated by the social structure, just as it was in the Hearn study. If the group climate is such that people do not mind being overheard, an open-office layout could enhance both general and intimate contact. For instance, the vice-president of a small company described the executive office:

> We decided to have both our desks in the same space, with a wall only half-way across. The president and I are in much better touch with what we are doing as a top management team. We know what commitments and contacts are being made. But it wouldn't work if we hadn't decided at the beginning not to have secrets from one another!

RELATIVE LOCATIONS

On a slightly larger scale, interaction is also affected by the relative locations of different facilities, people, and activity areas. For instance, social-group membership is heavily influenced by location. In a study conducted in a married-student housing project, Festinger, Schachter, and Back (1950) found that friendship patterns were affected by two major factors – sheer distance between houses (a separation of four or five seemed to be about the limit for friendship), and the direction in which the houses, and therefore their entrances, faced. People in houses whose entrances faced each other on a court tended to become a cohesive social group. People whose house fronts were turned (for aesthetic reasons) toward the street had less than half as many friends in the project as did those who lived in houses facing the courtyard. The investigators also found that people who lived near entries, stairways, and mailboxes made more friends and had a more active social life.

I have observed the same phenomenon at my Vermont home. The people that live next to the mailboxes (which are all in one location) have described to me their feeling of centrality in the community. The same effect is common in work organizations, where some people's work areas are in higher-contact locations than those of others. One girl I interviewed recognized this effect most clearly after her situation had changed:

> My social life has changed drastically since my desk was moved to the end of a corridor. I used to be right near the entrance to the whole place, and saw almost everyone as they came in and out. I don't have so many interruptions now, but I also have fewer conversations. I also eat lunch by myself more, when groups forget to include me. I like the whole feeling less than before.

Another locational factor that influences interaction is the presence or absence of central gathering spaces – places that are not "owned" by anyone but are likely to be used by many members of a system or community. A good setting for accidental or informal contact needs several characteristics. First, the setting must be central, that is, people must pass through it on their way to other places. Second, there must be places to sit or rest. Third, people must be able to stop in the setting to converse or watch others without blocking the flow of vehicular or foot traffic. A bulletin board in a busy narrow hallway, for example, is almost useless, since no one can stop long enough to read it or chat with others about the notices without clogging up the whole hallway.

An example of a good central space is Sproule Plaza at the University of California at Berkeley. In addition to the factors mentioned above, good weather increases the comfort of just "hanging around." I am convinced that this space was a major factor in the community contacts that led to the Free Speech Movement. Even though the demonstrators complained of alienation from the huge university, they were able to come together for common action in ways that most student bodies never do.

This coming together would have been much more difficult, if not impossible, without Sproule Plaza.

The nature of work tasks and their associated technologies often affect the locations in which people do their work and thereby also influence the amount of social contact. Early in this book I described the Hawthorne experiment, in which the single room set up for the work promoted contact among the members of the group. The opposite effect often occurs as well. Blauner (1964) describes a miners' union in England that demanded "hazard pay" when changes in work technology required the miners to work in isolation from one another. The point was not just that physical danger increased, but also that it was psychologically more stressful to work alone.

Finally, location plays a part not only when people are isolated *from* one another, but also when they are isolated *with* one another for long periods of time. Altman and Haythorn (1967) found that experimental pairs in isolation from all other contacts developed specific patterns of interpersonal contact that helped them maintain a manageable climate during their forced interaction. Territorial behavior with bed and chair (identifying a piece of furniture as exclusively one's own) tended to reduce conflicts; those pairs that did not develop territorial norms tended to last a shorter time in the experiment than those that did.

Topics of conversation are also influenced by isolation. As a submarine officer put it:

> On a two-month cruise, certain topics are just not talked about, as a way of keeping friction down. I found this out the hard way by being more vocal since I wasn't a career officer. I learned after my first cruise, though. You know you've got to be with those guys for a long time, it's just not worth it to take the chance of a permanent blow-up.

Other occupational groups – polar explorers, weather station personnel, and oil explorers – have reported the same self-monitoring of group behavior. I have heard a family describe the same process when they were on a camping trip. It is clear that forced interaction in a closed setting has a big influence on the quality of social contact that occurs.

MOBILITY

The last effect of settings on social contact that I will discuss here is the extent to which physical mobility is allowed or required. In general, the freer people are to move around, the more likely they are to come in contact with one another, especially if they are not next to each other in their regular seats or work stations.

The nature of the technology of a particular kind of work often has a major impact on physical mobility. For instance, Blauner (1964) points out that on automobile assembly lines the combination of noise and fixed work positions produces a sense of powerlessness in the workers and inhibits group formation. The operators have very little contact with their co-workers as long as the belt is bringing work to them in a steady flow.[3] He contrasts this with automated chemical process plants, where operators are free to move as they choose. They have both greater contact with other operators and more opportunity to see where their work fits into the whole process of the plant. However, there are also limits on mobility, as one can see from Blauner's description of textile workers tending "acres" of machines in an automated plant. The workers have great mobility but little real freedom to interact with one another, since they must move swiftly to deal with problems on a large number of machines. They have only fleeting contact with one another, although this is slightly more than they would have if they were locked into one position. Both a lack of mobility and forced mobility can reduce contact.

One of the most interesting examples of the impact of mobility on social contact is the new 747 jumbo jet. The increased size has allowed more aisle space and the inclusion of lounge areas. This change in physical setting has increased mobility, with some interesting social effects:

> In flight, passengers behave differently on board a jumbo than on a smaller jet. "A gregariousness has set in that we did not reckon on," says Pan Am president Najeeb Halaby. Passengers wander up and down the two aisles, try to help the stewardessess, or invade the first-class flight lounge on the deck.[4]

The most important long-run effect of increased jet size may well be on the nature of air travel as a social experience, rather than simply on the number of people carried per trip.

---

3 R. Blauner, *Alienation and Freedom*, Chicago: University of Chicago Press, 1964, p. 114.

4 "Jumbo Beats the Gremlins," *Time*, July 13, 1970.

CHOICE ABOUT CONTACT

I would like to close this section on settings and social contact with the question of how you decide whether the social effects of a particular setting are good. This depends upon who the users are, what they want in the way of contact, and what the relevant social system needs in the way of minimum contact of members in order to survive.

For instance, let us return for a moment to the case of the 747 jet. Zinsser (1970) raises some questions (which I share) about whether the new layout may *force* contact and remove the traveler's choice to be alone if he wishes.

> But all that we really want from the 747 is to get there in reasonable comfort and to be left alone – just what we always wanted from the ocean liners and never got . . . Perhaps we should want it otherwise. As the number of our fellow passengers increases, so should our ability to enjoy their company and to feel a little less alone. Yet when all is said (by the pilot) and done (by the stewardess), flight is still a solitary encounter with our own emotions.[5]

In other words, the limited mobility on earlier planes allowed many people who preferred solitude to get it with little effort. Now that movement around the plane is easier, the "solitaries" will have to work harder to maintain their aloneness – the space is not helping them as much.

Decisions about settings design and the resulting contact are usually made by someone who has a particular vested interest in the outcome. Sommer (1969) provides a graphic example:

> Cafe patrons around the world may be in for an unpleasant surprise. Furniture designer Henning Larsen was consulted by Copenhagen cafe owners whose customers lingered endlessly over coffee. Larsen developed a chair that exerts disagreeable pressure on the spine if occupied for over a few minutes. The Larsen chair is now being marketed in New York and other cities.[6]

W. Zinsser, "As Jumbo Jets Arrive and Liners Depart, Must Shuffleboard Roll On Forever?" *Life*, January 23, 1970. Reprinted by permission.

R. Sommer, *Personal Space, op. cit.*, p. 121. Reprinted by permission.

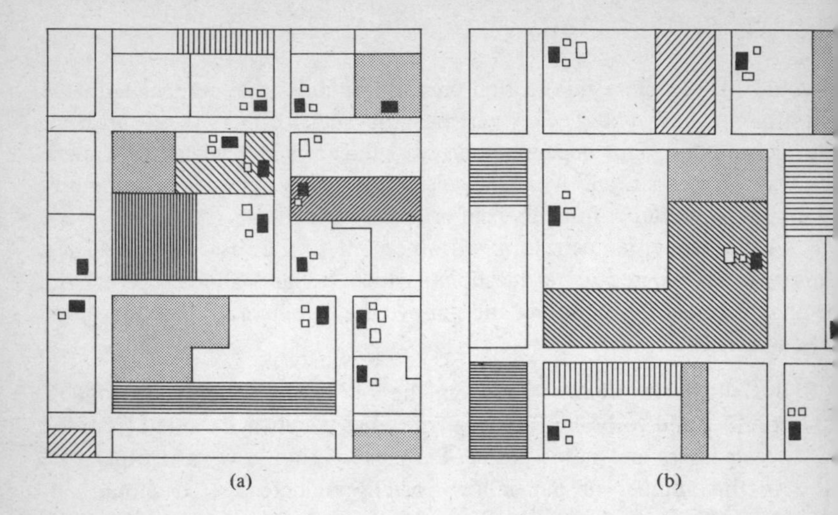

Fig. 5.2 Relative locations of farmhouses in (a) Quebec and (b) western Kansa

We could well expect the Larsen chair to show up in company lounge where employees take their breaks. The point is that the chair would b ordered by the office management, not by the employees who would b using it. Similarly, the cafe owners, not the patrons, decided tha prolonged conversation was not desirable. A similar process occurs wit the *use* of existing structures. I recently heard of a new midwestern hig school that was designed with a very effective central forum. Earl experiences in the new school showed that the central forum was used as catch-all gathering place, much as the Sproule Plaza I described earlie This interaction, however, was a threat to the administration of the schoo given the nature of the shaky relationship between authority and student in schools today. To keep students from getting together too long, th administration now stations staff members in the forum to move student along. "Hanging out" in a perfect hanging-out space has been outlawed.

Finally, it is sometimes hard to tell where *preferences* for a particula level of social contact leave off and the *effects* of particular settings o those preferences begin. A person may prefer a certain intensity of contac with others because he has spent long periods in a setting that provide that kind of contact. The example given earlier of Americans' preference for private rooms and offices fits this pattern.

Another striking example was revealed to me as I happened to fly over Quebec and western Kansas on two successive days. In Quebec the pattern of farmhouses was like diagram (*A*) in Fig. 5.2, whereas the pattern in Kansas was like (*B*). These patterns suggested two things. First, it seemed that the French-Canadian farmers preferred more immediate, easy contact with their neighbors than did the Kansans. Second, these patterns once again raised the question of cause and effect. Each present group of farmers probably grew up in the type of setting it now experiences; the farmers' early examples of what life and contact should be like were conditioned by what it *was* like.

In other words, over a long time period, the setting influences our experiences and makes us feel comfortable with and prefer certain kinds of social contact. These preferences then influence the way we choose and structure our settings, so that the influence of the person-setting process is circular.

6
FUNCTION III: SYMBOLIC IDENTIFICATION

This function is concerned with the extent to which a setting provides information about the nature of the people who are connected with it. The key question is: What does this place and its facilities tell us about the people who use or own it – about their values, goals, personal preferences, and the like? This is the most basic form of the communication function of space.

The test for the symbolic identification dimension is what information a setting conveys about the nature of the individuals or groups connected with it. As such, the emphasis is on what the setting *actually* tells a perceiver, not on what the owner or user *intends* to communicate about himself (although that is an interesting comparison in its own right).

Even though this information can be useful for task and other purposes, I also see it as an important function for its own sake. People have a need to know with whom they are dealing, as a way of defining their world, not simply as a means to some other end. I make this distinction for practical as well as theoretical reasons. Spatial decisions in organizations are often made for symbolic reasons, even when they are rationalized as task-oriented. When new office furniture is ordered another large desk may be purchased even though the user's need for an area for spreading out papers has shrunk to almost nothing. The symbolic use of space quickly becomes an end in itself.

In the following discussion, I will describe three types of spatial symbolic identification. One is information about the nature of an organization or group as a social system. The second is messages about a person's relationship to (and position in) a social system. The third is information about a person and his characteristics.

INFORMATION ABOUT THE SYSTEM

All the physical facilities of an organization make a statement about the nature of that social system. These facilities are a physical record of the choices that the managers have made about how to shape the system and what to have around it. The most fundamental choice is *where to locate* the organization physically. This decision speaks volumes about how people in the organization see themselves, as well as about how they want others to see them. Many corporations maintain their headquarters in mid-town Manhattan or in the Wall Street area at great economic and psychic cost in order to project an image of reliability and high quality to both members and customers.

Just as locating in the suburbs says something different from locating in the central city, locating in a run-down area gives a different message than locating in an expensive, well-maintained section of the city. This has been discovered the hard way by many community service agencies. For example, one agency has found that its choice to locate in a well-to-do area, while comfortable for the members of the system and gratifying to their status needs, reduces the agency's relevant identity with their clients, most of whom are poor and do not feel at ease in that location. The poor take the location as an important piece of information about whether the agency will be able to identify with them and their problems. This problem of location has led many organizations engaged in community development to adopt "storefront" locations. The nature of the storefront itself is not nearly so important as *where* it is and the fact that it *is* a storefront rather than a fancy office.

The second major way a system communicates its identity is through the *attributes* of its facilities. A very simple example is the visible difference in values between a firm that has early American decoration and furniture (stability, tradition, "America first," consistency) and one that uses an amalgamation of new styles (change, experimentation, "with it," variety). These settings project differing images to the people who enter the systems.

Organizations often put considerable energy and thought into generating a suitable identity. Manning (1965) provides a nice example of this in a general manager's statement:

> If I may use a rather hackneyed phrase, we wanted to impress an "image" on the people of Manchester and elsewhere of the strength and size of the CIS through the medium of a modern office building. Very few people see our balance sheet or read our chairman's report but this new building will be a constant reminder that the CIS is a large and first-class insurance office. We have already made use of the model in our advertising material and hope to extend this when the building is completed. We believe that these new premises will have an impact upon our staff, including the senior staff, by giving them a feeling of pride.[1]

This is a very perceptive statement on two counts. First, a company's physical facilities are more concrete and visible than its workings or social structure, and are, therefore, the most immediate means of communicating an image to the public at large. Second, a system's facilities communicate not only to outsiders, but to members of the system as well. Insiders get a sense of what their organization is like from their offices. This may even help them behave more in line with the image the building projects, much as people tend to behave like religious persons when they enter an impressive church.

Physical facilities also communicate information about the social structure of an organization, particularly about the relative status or centrality of different subunits within the system. For instance, my work as consultant to personnel departments has made it very clear to me that members of most organizations feel the personnel function to be of low potency and importance. The personnel offices are usually cramped, very inelegantly furnished (read "drab" if you like), and located in out-of-the-way or "leftover" space. The symbolic significance of this is all the greater because in many systems the personnel department is visited more frequently by both current and prospective employees than any other department. The setting of a personnel department should be quite carefully designed; in fact it is usually not, in keeping with its low status in the system.

---

1 P. Manning, *Office Design: A Study of Environment*. Liverpool, England: The Pilkington Research Unit, 1965. Reprinted by permission.

Certain aspects of a system may be designed to communicate specifically to the outside public. You can often tell what image an organization wants to project by comparing two similar places, one of which is used only by insiders, and the other by both insiders and the public. For instance, in one television station the hallway used by the audience to get into the studio is decorated in good taste, with visual displays of various station features. The overall impact is of a colorful, artistic, and active station. By contrast, the hallway where performers and scenery enter the studio are wide but stark, with absolutely no color or decoration. The administrators clearly feel that since the workers already know that the station is active, they do not need visual reminders. However, a more likely possibility is that the audience hallway was designed by the public relations department to be specifically symbolic, whereas the work hallway was designed by the props department for movement of large pieces of scenery, with no thought to the symbolic effect on the people who also have to pass through there.

Of course, it is not just individual organizations that communicate their identity through their physical structures. Whole societies symbolize the nature of their various institutions through their architecture. The national monuments in Washington are the purest symbolic examples we have in this country. The Lincoln, Washington, and Jefferson memorials manage to say both that the history of our country is based on the efforts of great individuals and that the greatness of the country is larger than individuals – the latter being communicated by the scale of the monuments. This effect is not limited to purely symbolic monuments, however. We build many of our public buildings to communicate the same sense of the size and importance of society: courts, prisons, government buildings such as the Pentagon, banks, and so on.

Structures are also built for their effect on future generations. Albert Speer (1970) provides a good example from 20th century Germany:

> Hitler liked to say that the purpose of his building was to transmit his time and its spirit to posterity. Ultimately, all that remained to remind men of the great epochs of history was their monumental architecture, he would philosophize. What had remained of the emperors of Rome? What would still bear witness to them today, if their buildings had not survived?[2]

---

2 A. Speer, *Inside the Third Reich*, p. 65. Copyright © 1969 by Verlaz Ullstein GMBH; copyright © 1970 by The Macmillan Company.

Note a not uncommon phenomenon: Hitler's symbolic purpose would slide from communicating about the *times* and their spirit, to bearing witness to the *emperors* themselves. More than one office building has been built to testify to the power and glory of the man who authorized the funds.

THE INDIVIDUAL IN THE SYSTEM

The second type of symbolic identification is concerned with information about the individual's identity in the social system. Settings communicate information about a user's level in the formal hierarchy, the kinds of functions he performs for the system, how a visitor to the setting is expected to relate to the system, and many other person-to-system relationships.

The most familiar example of this type of identification is undoubtedly the "status symbol" in its traditional organizational use. Various facilities and patterns of facilities form the basis for a visual language by which insiders and knowledgeable outsiders can tell at a glance an individual's status level in the system. Some of the elements used as status indicators are:

–Size in square feet of personal space (more space usually signifies higher status).

–Luxuriousness of appointments (carpet, drapes, thickness of carpet).

–A private office (being less visible to others usually signifies higher status).

–Desk (having one, size, design, and materials out of which it is made).

–Location of office (on "executive row," in a central place, or in a "backwater," etc.).

–Windows (having one or more, distance to them).

–Decorations (quality, whether provided by company or not).

–Secretary (private one or sharing one with others).

–Location of secretary (in a pool, inside or outside one's office).

As I am sure most readers know, the list is as long as people's ingenuity in devising visual differentiations.

In practice, the visual signals may be quite subtle. For instance, Manning (1965) describes the facilities allocation in a new office building:

> The rank of "senior official" entitles the holder to a 3 X 3 module (approximately 240 sq. ft) office; the rank of "official" entitles its holder to a 3 X 2 module (approx. 160 sq. ft) office . . . The occupants of the 3 X 2 module office were given the choice of three complete decors but were not able to take part of one and part of another. Senior officials had a greater range of choice.[3]

In other words, the status difference between officials and senior officials was not in the *quality* of their furnishings, since they were from the same central supply, but rather in the degree of *variety* in decor, with higher members sending the signal that they were allowed more free choice in their combination of decorations.

Manning does not say whether there were rules against real variety, that is, against members bringing their own furnishings into their offices. I have found that in many organizations, personal furniture is a status symbol; only people at the highest levels are allowed to exercise that kind of personal choice.

On the other hand, the signals are usually fairly direct. The prize for directness of communication about position in the organization's hierarchy undoubtedly goes to an insurance company president, who chose the design of the building which is shown in Fig. 6.1. The building was described in *Newsweek* (1966):

> At Allgemeine Rechtsschutz AG, a West German insurance firm, employees will have unmistakable evidence of their standing on the corporate ladder when a new $2.8 million headquarters opens in Düsseldorf at the end of the year. Each story will be occupied by a progressively higher echelon of workers, from 360 typists and clerks on the ground floor to president Heinz G. Kramberg alone at the top on the twelfth floor. Kramberg says he ordered the staircase design to "encourage ambition and provide a visual image of our organization structure."[4]

Although the formal structure of the organization is not so visible in most office buildings as in president Kramberg's, the use of height to show

---

3 P. Manning, *op. cit.*, p. 474. Reprinted by permission.

4 "Stairway to Success." Copyright Newsweek, Inc., October 24, 1966, p. 99.

Fig. 6.1 The "stairway to success." (Photograph by Claus Wolde.)

hierarchical level is very common in the United States. If you plotted organizational level against floor level, the correlation would be very high for most corporate headquarters. And if you diagrammed the density (e.g., persons per given floor area) of successively higher floors, you would get a diagram that looks like Kramberg's building.

Although there are fairly general indicators, such as size of personal area, that tend to mean the same thing in most organizations, a consultant or visitor to a system should learn the specific symbolic language of that system if he intends to make any judgments based on status information. For instance, Hall (1966) provides a cross-cultural example:

> Americans do not normally distinguish in an operational way between the right and left side of the outer offices. Nor is the half that is

nearest the door differentiated from the inner half. Eastern Mediterranean Arabs do make formal distinctions – people sitting near the door are of lower status than those near the far wall. The right side of the room is for relatives, the left side is for nonrelatives.[5]

There are similar differences in the way different groups use room position in American firms. Homans (1950) noted that the workroom layout in the Hawthorne studies was used by members as a status indicator. Workers with the lowest-status jobs were relegated to the "back" of the room (away from the door), and as people acquired more prestigious jobs they moved toward the front of the room. Conversely, I found the opposite usage of room position in an investment firm. The lowest-status clerical workers were in the front rows of a large room. Slightly higher-status workers sat behind them, and so on, with the supervisor of the whole group at the very back. Since everyone's desk faced the front, formal status was also indicated by who could be seen; each person could see those who were below him in status, but could not see his superiors.

Settings also send messages to their users about a more inclusive process than status relative to other individual members; settings communicate about the relative importance of the individual in relation to the system as a whole. As I noted earlier, the existence or absence of personal effects in an individual's immediate area says something about the extent to which individuals in that social system can influence their own life space. The structure of a classroom in which the teacher's desk faces the students speaks clearly about how the system expects the student to see himself – one of the herd, nonspecial, and identityless when compared with the teacher, who has a unique, and often raised, place at the front of the room. (Even simple details can get this message across, as the Peanuts cartoon in Fig. 6.2 shows so well.)

The best example I have found of the use of space to make the individual feel insignificant in the system comes from Hitler's building plans. As Speer (1970) describes the entrance to the new Chancellery:

> It was to be a series of rooms done in a rich variety of materials and color combinations, in all some seven hundred twenty-five feet long. Only then came Hitler's reception hall. . . .

---

5 E. Hall, *The Hidden Dimension, op. cit.*, p. 44. Reprinted by permission.

Fig. 6.2 (© 1970 United Feature Syndicate, Inc.)

> Hitler was delighted. "On the long walk from the entrance to the reception hall they'll get a taste of the power and grandeur of the German Reich!" . . . Hitler was so well pleased with the long hike the diplomats had to take in the recently completed Chancellery that he wanted a similar device in the new building. I therefore doubled the distance visitors would have to traverse, making it somewhat more than a quarter of a mile.[6]

This design served to make both citizens and foreign visitors feel the difference in scale between the power of the Third Reich and their own lack of importance. Many modern office buildings seem designed to produce a very similar effect, for both members and outside visitors.

---

6 A. Speer, *op. cit.*, pp. 123, 187. Reprinted by permission.

Of course, settings also provide information about the functions and activities of those who use them. For example, in a dog food plant the meat processing rooms are very different in sight, touch, and smell from the plant engineer's area; and each is, in turn, different from the plant manager's office.

I would also like to note what most readers probably know from personal experience: that the symbolic representation of where people fit in the organization acquires a disproportionate importance in most work organizations. Issues related to status symbols and appropriate cues generate emotions far in excess of their actual importance to the work of the system. Everyone has his own favorite examples of this emotional investment; this is one of mine, as given to me by a friend:

> Recently our company built a new office building. Because of expanding staff, we also retained the use of the old building, with some shuffling of people to the new one. One lower level manager in the old building ended up in a small office with very meagre carpeting on the floor. However, since his particular level was not entitled to a carpet, his boss insisted that it be torn up – at considerable expense – and thrown away.

Finally, the importance placed upon physical indicators of a person's standing in the system varies from organization to organization, depending on the nature of the social climate. I believe that the social variable that most influences the amount of emphasis on status symbols is the extent to which people receive direct, concrete feedback about their standing and performance in the organization. A case described recently by a friend made this clearer to me:

> I'm one of a large group of young lawyers who came into the firm at about the same time. A few weeks ago I was told by the director to move to another office. It was purely because I need to be near another man for a long-term project we are developing, but nobody believed that. We get practically no information on how we're doing in the firm, so all the other guys at my level were trying to figure out what the move meant for them, and whether they should start looking for another job because I now have the "inside track."

In other words, given the low amount of feedback in the system and workers' assumption that moves are almost never made for task reasons, spatial events were read as part of the system's communication about everyone's standing – even when the move was not meant to carry that kind of message. This example also suggests that symbolic status indicators will be considered particularly important in organizations that have large groups of people without much formal differentiation in positional level. If formal job descriptions do not provide a "pecking order," then other cues will be relied upon to fulfill this function.

THE INDIVIDUAL

Our final type of symbolic identification is the information provided by physical settings about the nature of the individual: his interests, values, personal tastes, interpersonal style, and so on. We get this information from the way people structure and influence their immediate personal areas, e.g., their desks or offices. We can read statements about a person from his choice of decorations, the ways in which he arranges his furniture (to allow people to come close to him or to keep them away, for instance), and the kinds of things he chooses to display (bowling trophies, pictures of his family, prints of sailing ships, avant-garde minimalist sculpture, etc.). Families are well aware of this communication process when they move into a new house. Often, their first acts are to put up curtains, mow the lawn, and the like – acts that are aimed in large part at communicating to the neighbors that the new residents are the right kind of people for the neighborhood.

To read something about a person from his immediate setting does not require, however, that he had others in mind when he made his choices. We often arrange our facilities simply because we like them that way, which is in a sense communicating to ourselves about who we are and what we like. Also, a person need not take elaborate steps in "fixing up" his office area. Even his choice of how much energy he puts into arranging his office tells us something about his interests. Not everyone has the same degree of concern about his surroundings, but everyone *has* surroundings, and symbolic messages come from how he chooses to deal with these surroundings.

One qualification that must be made is the necessity of knowing *whose choices* we are seeing when we try to read something about an individual from his setting. Organizations vary with respect to the extent to which they allow members to influence their own settings. The greater the control exercised by the system, the less reliable the inferences we can make from physical cues about what the members are like as individuals. Where the system has more say than the person about his work space, however, people may sometimes point this out. As I walked into a luxuriously decorated, early American office, its occupant said sheepishly, "This is the position – it's not really me . . .," and indeed his office contained few items that had not been selected by the company.

The more a person does influence his own surroundings, however, through decoration, personal artifacts, rearrangement, bringing in his own furniture, and the like, the more data he provides about who he is. A visitor can then get information fairly quickly about similarities and differences between himself and the occupant of the place. This can be a help in establishing a new relationship, since it provides more data about what realistic expectations the visitor may have of the occupant, and it may stimulate the visitor to disclose more information about himself than he would if they were in some anonymous place, starting from zero information.

Whether the provision of personal data in an office setting is good or bad depends, however, on what the person is trying to do and to whom he is trying to relate. For instance, a social worker who is clever about decorating her office with personal artifacts that have meaning for her made an interesting observation. She said that the very personal quality of her office seemed to create a gulf between her and many of her clients. They were made painfully aware of the differences in means and skills between themselves and the social worker. If the clients were confident and at ease, usually they could use these visible differences in a positive way, for their own and the social worker's learning. But if they were not self-confident, the visible differences acted as a barrier to the development of a helpful relationship.

I saw the same thing happen recently when a middle manager visited an advertising executive's office. The manager reported that he was "really turned off by the Chianti bottles and the crazy drawings on the walls – I just couldn't relate to the guy." We might suspect that the manager's lack of confidence made him unable to use constructively the signals of difference between himself and the advertising man.

Finally, people send data about themselves not only from the way they structure settings, but also from the ways in which the settings are *used*. If a person walks freely through different spaces, he is telling himself and others that he has confidence and belongs there. Another example came from a consultant who told me that he always tried to move something, such as a chair or an ashtray when he went into another man's office, just to indicate that although not in his own territory, he was on an equal footing with the occupant. Similarly, a teacher told me that when he is working with a group of military people, he moves something in the lecture room before he starts, in order to establish the "correct" set of his being in charge. A salesman described to me the same process for establishing his control in customers' homes.

HISTORICAL MEANING

In discussing the impact of settings on symbolic identification of the system, the person in the system, and the individual, most of my examples have related to either the way facilities are constructed and arranged or the ways people are using them when observed. Another interesting way in which places communicate symbolically is through the events that have occurred in a setting. Over time, peoples' reactions to a place are based partly on its present shape and partly on their memories of what has happened there before. A formal board room says something to its users about themselves and the system, not just because it looks like a board room, but also because of the memories it triggers of earlier events and decisions made in it.

A powerful example of the symbolic impact of the physical properties and historical implications of the President's office is given by Neustadt (1960):

> Few men – and exceedingly few Cabinet officers – are immune to the impulse to say "yes" to the President of the United States. It grows harder to say "no" when they are seated in his oval office at the White House, or in his study on the second floor, where almost tangibly he partakes of the aura of his physical surroundings.[7]

A training director provides another example of the way events influence the meaning a place acquires:

> We tried holding these self-development seminars in our regular seminar room at the office, but it just didn't work. Everybody had had some previous experience in that room with some formal, official

---

7 R. Neustadt, *Presidential Power*, p. 34. Copyright © 1960 John Wiley. By permission of John Wiley and Sons, Inc.

> presentation or "show-and-tell" to higher management. The walls just seem to ooze messages saying that the appropriate behavior there is to look good and not take risks. The climate defined too much of how they should behave, and it wasn't what we wanted for these sessions, so we rented space off-site.

In other words, past events in the company's room sent signals about how people who are using it should behave in the present. Depending on the situation this can be an advantage, as the President's getting agreement, or a disadvantage, as the President's not hearing useful, important disagreements.

ACCURACY OF MESSAGE

My final point is that physical settings do not always contain messages that are accurate in terms of the realities of the social system. Subordinates often are quite clear that the boss's "open door" is a symbol of free contact only in his mind, and that one had better not go *through* that open door too often.

Parkinson (1957) provides a beautiful statement of how a misleading physical message applies to the organization as a whole:

> The institutions already mentioned (a research firm and a busy airport) – lively and productive as they may be – flourish in such shabby and makeshift surroundings that we might turn with relief to an institution clothed from the outset with convenience and dignity. The outer door, in bronze and glass, is placed centrally in a symmetric facade. Polished shoes glide quietly over shining rubber to the glittering and silent elevator . . . A minute later, and you are ankle deep in the director's carpet, plodding sturdily toward his distant, tidy desk. Hypnotized by the chief's unwavering stare, cowed by the Matisse hung upon his wall, you will feel that you have found real efficiency at last.
>
> In point of fact you will have discovered nothing of the kind. It is now known that a perfection of planned layout is achieved only by institutions on the point of collapse.[8]

---

8 C. Parkinson, *Parkinson's Law and Other Studies in Administration*. Boston: Houghton Mifflin, 1957, pp. 80-82. Reprinted by permission.

This phenomenon may not occur quite as often as Parkinson implies, but his point is well taken; systems often shape themselves physically to describe what they *wish* they were (e.g., an "open-office" layout in a system where people are closed with one another), or what they *used* to be (an efficient, energetic image when the system is running down). The messages of a system's spaces must be tested against one's experiences with the system and its actual workings.

7
FUNCTION IV: TASK INSTRUMENTALITY

The focus of this function of settings is on their usefulness for the accomplishment of tasks being performed within them. Examples of questions asked when this dimension is being rated are: How good is the fit between this kitchen and the cooking activities taking place in it? Are the layout and facilities of this workshop adequate for our cabinet-making activities? Am I free to do the kinds of things in this office that I need to do in order to accomplish my job goals?

In order to rate a setting on task instrumentality, we must first specify the tasks that are being performed there. In order to simplify the rating process, I have broken down tasks into three categories of component activities: physical activities that take place *outside* people, interactional activities that take place *between* people, and mental activities that occur *within* people.

PHYSICAL ACTIVITIES

There are many different physical task activities: machine operation, sanding, painting, lifting, moving around, sawing, hammering, rolling dough, and so on. The list is as long as man's history of production for his basic and peripheral needs. To illustrate the impact of settings on work, I have selected a number of attributes that affect task activities: size of work spaces, qualities of the materials in a place, technological features, sensory conditions, and flexibility.

Size of Work Place

The size of a work place is a major factor limiting what can be done there. If a desk is too small to spread papers out on, information will be available only sequentially (as the employee shuffles through the papers) rather than simultaneously (if the papers are all laid out in one place).

As another example, an artist friend told me that he finally moved to an old barn because he realized that the scale of his work was controlled by the size of his small studio. His choices had been determined more by the space available than by the artistic problems he was trying to solve.

This example is similar to the problem many television stations have, particularly those occupying older buildings. The scale of the scenery that can be used is limited by the size of the elevators, hallways, and doors. One TV executive described some anxious moments his group had when they were trying to get an automobile into the studio to display as the prize for a game show. They were going to have to do the show in another city, with a revenue loss to the original station, until they hit upon the solution of cutting the automobile in two parts, right down the center of the hood, and taping it together on the stage.[1]

The Quality of Materials

The quality of materials used in a setting strongly influences what can be done there. For instance, if a place is built with heavy structural materials such as thick, concrete floors, then work on large, heavy items can be done there. Otherwise, heavy work will deteriorate the floor rapidly. Similarly, a floor that is easily damaged by grease and other substances is a great drawback in a meat-processing area, just as it is in household kitchens.

The nature of materials is an influence in office areas, especially with respect to the materials used in wall and partition surfaces. If these are plaster, painted sheetrock, or are otherwise easily damaged, the occupants are inhibited in their use of the area. They tend to feel that they must not mar the walls by using tape or nails to hang up pictures, etc. As a result,

---

1 Yes, the winner did get a different car.

the place will be less personal, since people have less influence on it and put up fewer things of their own. Such surfaces also limit some work efforts such as using walls for quick visual display of newsprint or other large papers. The more damageable the construction materials, the more restricted the activities people will feel free to carry out there.

In contrast to a completely finished effect, the walls of the studio in my house at Prickley Mountain are of painted plywood and spruce siding, i.e., surfaces which can be repainted, nailed into, taped, etc., without any deterioration. In fact, all these "damaging" acts enhance the richness of the walls by providing a record of past activities. I believe that organizations could follow similar lines with many of their office areas if they could first reduce their love for traditionally slick and clean, but inhibiting, materials.

The most widespread instance of materials' inhibiting physical activities is that of the settings which we carry around from place to place, i.e., our clothes. Clothes form a very close, portable environment which serves several functions – shelter, symbolic identification, and task. A millworker's heavy-duty overalls carry out all three functions well by protecting him from flying chips, sending a clear, accurate message about his role and the kind of work he does, and allowing him free movement for his lifting and pushing activities. The overalls are not easily damaged and do not need to remain unspotted, even though detergent manufacturers would like to convince wives otherwise. This allows him psychological freedom of movement, since he is not concerned about the effect of his activities on his clothes.

In contrast, most uniforms in the white-collar occupations (even the name signifies it) are worn mainly for symbolic reasons. The gray-flannel suit identifies the wearer as a well-meaning and well-groomed member in good standing with the organization. His clothes must also be clean and pressed. All of these tend to restrict movement and limit the kinds of activities that a person will engage in while at work. It may be, for instance, that people do not change their work areas around very much partly because they do not want to muss their clothes. These people will also tend to avoid certain areas, such as a dusty room in the plant, in order to remain neat and clean.

One means for highlighting how inhibiting our styles of organizational dress really are would be to have everyone in a system wear sweatsuits to work for a few days so that they could see how their behavior changes. So far no work group has been willing to take me up on this.

Technological Features

The technological features of a setting obviously influence what can be done there. A mill room set up with both a planer to cut boards and a sander to do finish work requires less movement of men and wood than does a setup with these two machines in separate rooms. In many American organizations, the key technological question is whether the office or plant layout provides adequate facilities for communication and reception of information. Mogulescu (1970) conveys this aspect very well in his description of the up-to-date board room.

> Included in the room is a special console that flashes programmed slides, films, and other visuals onto an integrated three-part screen-wall. Behind the screen-wall is a control room equipped with the full range of the most advanced communications tools. As befits the board room of a leading business machines manufacturer, there is a built-in computer that allows members, at the touch of a button, to see the latest data projected on the screen-wall for their immediate use. Meetings are also automatically tape-recorded and board proceedings are instantly available for replay.[2]

Actually, I also get from this description a sense that the technology is serving symbolic as well as task functions by indicating that the company is indeed up-to-date. But that does not negate the fact that the facilities are available to be used, and many groups' modes of operation have changed as a result of having facilities available with which to experiment.

Sensory Conditions

The sensory conditions of a place are the "human factors" aspect of the environment: temperature, humidity, light, noise, freshness of air, and so on. These factors have a strong influence on the kinds of activities that can be carried out in a place, as well as on how well those activities can be performed. I discovered a company in Maine that has operated for 45 years with no heating system in the plant. In the wintertime, as the men describe it, one can do only those tasks that keep one moving enough to generate strong body heat. The more stationary tasks wait until spring. Caplan and Lindsay (1946) found that at the opposite end of the

---

2 M. Mogulescu, *op. cit.*, p. 70. Reprinted by permission.

temperature scale, miners' performance dropped off as a function of heat and humidity and that the reduction was greatest in the third hour of a three-hour shift. In other words, the impact of bad environmental conditions is especially critical when it coincides with a person's internal blockages, such as fatigue.

Orwell (1937) provides another mining example in a very moving description of the trip required to get to the working seam of an English mine:

> Before I had been down a mine I had vaguely imagined the miner stepping out of the cage and getting to work on a ledge of coal a few yards away. I had not realized that before he even gets to his work he may have to creep through passages as long as from London Bridge to Oxford Circus . . . Usually it is bad going underfoot – thick dust or jagged chunks of shale, and in some mines where there is water it is as mucky as a farmyard . . . At the start to walk stooping is rather a joke, but it is a joke that soon wears off. I am handicapped by being exceptionally tall, but when the roof falls to four feet or less, it is a tough job for anybody except a dwarf or a child. You have not only got to bend double, you have also got to keep your head up all the while so as to see the beams and girders and dodge them when they come. You have, therefore, a constant crick in your neck, but this is nothing compared to the pain in your knees and thighs.[3]

The conditions for the miners' job are in large part determined by two things: the method used to get the coal, and the resulting journey that must be made to get to the work area. A tremendous toll is taken in spirit and energy just to get to the work in that setting, let alone in the heavy labor in close, hot, dusty, cramped spaces.

Control of environmental conditions produces the opposite situation in most office buildings today. Light, temperature, air circulation, and humidity are all controlled inside the building, no matter what the outside climate is like. Of course, efforts at environmental control can still go awry, as in Le Corbusier's design for the government buildings at Chandigar, India. His sculpturally magnificent openings and passageways, built to provide air circulation, also circulate tons of dust through the offices. The dust was a feature of the local geography that apparently was

---

3 G. Orwell, *The Road to Wigan Pier*. New York: Harcourt Brace & World, 1937, pp. 33-34. Reprinted by permission.

not considered a crucial feature of the setting when the buildings were designed.

Flexibility

The flexibility of a setting determines whether a variety of activities can be carried on there, or only the activity for which it was designed. A factory operation with permanent assembly-line installations must usually redesign its space in order to change the nature of its tasks. A job shop with equipment on rollers, on the other hand, changes shape with the ebb and flow of customer requests. The job shop uses this flexibility to advantage in terms of shorter reaction time to new task demands.

Similarly, office areas vary on the flexibility dimension. Many rooms are designed for only one purpose, e.g., the board room, and therefore are not utilized much of the time.[4] University classrooms in which the seats are bolted to the floor in one fixed arrangement are convenient for the cleaning people, but are not very useful for learning activities other than lectures. As Sommer (1969) points out, the task of organizational design is to create settings that are neither so amorphous that nothing can be done well there, nor so inflexibly specific that the setting cannot be used for changing tasks and needs.

ACTIVITIES WITH INTERACTION

Some task activities require human interaction: selling merchandise or service to customers, checking out information with someone else, meeting in a group to identify or decide work issues, trading ideas that stimulate new directions of thought, and so on. The emphasis here is on interaction as a means to task accomplishment, rather than as an end in itself (which was the focus of the social contact dimension). I will illustrate a selected number of aspects of settings that influence task interaction. These are distance of work places from one another, size of available meeting spaces interference factors, technological organization of the work, and flexibility of location.

---

4 This is another example of pseudo-fixed-feature space, where the room could be used for multiple purposes, but this is not allowed for symbolic reasons (the room is saved for those who "deserve" it).

Distance

Distance between work areas has the effect of reducing people's task interaction. Allen (1969) found in his studies of technical information-sharing in a research laboratory, a medical laboratory, and a management school that the frequency of a person's communication with his colleagues in the office was a function of the distance between the desks. Frequency of communication declined as a direct function of the square of the distance between the two desks.

Allen also found that contact was correlated negatively with "the amount of difficulty, by way of corners to be turned, indirect paths to be followed, etc., encountered in traversing a path" from one person's desk to another. Although he calls this the "nuisance factor," I prefer to think of it as the *functional distance* between people at work. In many office layouts the distance between desks often seems much greater psychologically than the separation in feet. The following excerpt, a manager's description of how he sees the route to his boss's office, may be one of the more extreme examples of functional distance:

> I go from my office out past the receptionist and down the hall to the other end of the building. I take the elevator to 12, get off, and take another one to 21. I get off and walk to the other end of the building, turn and pass through three doors, and I'm at his office – about 100 feet straight above where I started!

The effect of this is obvious and fits with Allen's finding. As the manager commented drily, "We don't see each other nearly as often as we should."

Distance also keeps whole groups from interacting with each other. The history of relations between the home office and the field location is filled with examples of long-distance separation leading to infrequent contact which, in turn, leads to distorted pictures of the other group. When central-office people do go into the field, they are often given the kind of picture which the field wants to portray. As one plant manager described it to me:

> We work out a "grand tour" which shows them the good sides, exposes one or two small problems that we can ask their advice on, and gets them the hell out of here before they can really dig into all the ways we have to do things here that don't fit "policy."

The distance from the home office allows the field people enough time to set up their props, so in that sense distance helps them. However, if there were less separation, the field people probably would not think of themselves as so distinct from the administrative center of the organization, and there would be less need for careful image management.

The Size of Meeting Spaces

The size of meeting spaces has a fairly direct effect on task interaction. For instance, small conference rooms tend to promote a pattern of small-group meetings on a problem, even at stages when a much larger group would be more appropriate. The task suffers when the meeting size is determined by the size of the room, not by the magnitude of the problem.

Most organizations that I have observed have no large gathering spaces where some significant percentage of the people in the system can meet at one time. I have found this to be a drawback in some of my own organization development work. When I want to hold a large-scale briefing or exercise that will involve many of the organization's members, I usually have to find some hotel meeting room because no such space exists inside the system. This is unfortunate for two reasons. First, we are then out of the system's day-to-day spaces; if we were meeting on the system's home ground, the event could also influence how the people use their facilities day to day. Second, I hope to start a pattern of social work-oriented events that are more varied than the usual patterns of organizational interaction. If spaces are not available in the system, more planning effort is required, and large-scale gatherings will tend not to occur at the initiative of the system itself, but only through the prompting of an outside consultant.

Of course, spaces may also be *too big* for the interactions which are supposed to take place in them. Many board rooms that I have seen have this characteristic, especially if the size of the ever-present table forces people to be distant from one another, although that is not the mood they are trying to foster. I recently saw an interesting solution to the scale problem in a nonoffice setting, a jazz nightclub. Two folding walls at right angles to each other were installed in the main room, permitting management to change both the width and the length of the room to fit the size of the audience and the mood of the music being played.

Interference Factors

Those aspects of the setting which interfere with interaction are called interference factors: noise, heavy traffic flow, noxious smells, and so on. For instance, if a plant is very noisy, operators often cannot hear one another when they are trying to communicate about a crisis. They are reduced to the much more limited vocabulary of hand signals to pass on vital information, and decisions can be slowed or made impossible in this process.

Similarly, meetings that take place in an area where other people pass through have two strikes against them from the beginning. The movement of people produces visual as well as auditory distractions, and this sense of reduced privacy often limits what information the members of the meeting will feel free to share with one another.

Technological Organization of Work

A fourth factor having an impact on the amount and kinds of task interaction that workers will have is the technological organization of the work. The developers of the sociotechnical systems approach to work analysis have demonstrated quite clearly that tasks can be organized in alternative ways which have different impacts on the interaction and social system of the workers. In their evaluation of the change from short-wall to long-wall coal mining methods, Trist *et al.* (1963) demonstrated how the new technology separated men of different skill operations from one another, even though the men depended on one another for completion of the cycle. The result was that "no overall social organization exists to bind these segregated groups together in common pursuit of the primary task of completing the cycle."[5]

For a similar effect, we can consider an example from a system where the primary task is learning. A colleague had just visited a new conference center, which he described to me as follows:

> It has all the latest gadgets in it – movable screens, cameras, projectors, rolling blackboards, sensers that people can push to provide answers (a) – (e) for multiple choice questions. It's a big lecture hall with all the seats in tiered rows, bolted down and facing the podium down in the pit. They are very proud of it as "psychological architecture." Personally, I think it's based on an inadequate theory of how learning takes place, so it's no better than a haphazard design.

---

5 E. Trist and E. Bamforth, "Some Social and Psychological Consequences of the Long-wall Method of Coal-Getting," *Human Relations* 4, 1951, p. 46.

The major impact of this technology was to reinforce a passive relationship: the audience received information from an authoritative source operating from either the front of the room or the control center. The structure made it very difficult for interaction among the learners. I, like my friend, believe that this is a great handicap to most kinds of learning.

Flexibility of Location

Flexibility of location for people's work space is particularly useful when tasks and therefore interaction needs are changing over time. For instance, in systems engaged in highly technical problem-solving, the project team has become a popular form of temporary organization. People from different functional areas are identified as a working team for the life of a specific project. When that project is completed they are assigned to a new team or return to specialist work within their functional area. One factor in the success of this process of organization is the physical location of the team members. In one system, project team members kept their locations in their functional areas, even though their assignments to different teams changed quite frequently. However, the teams had difficulty in forming, members reported that the problems they were working on were not well defined and in general, the interaction of team members was less than that needed for effective operation.

Allen (1969) makes a similar point in his analysis of technical information sharing. He suggests that short-term project teams should be located in one area for quick contact, except in instances where technical obsolescence can occur very quickly. He points out that in this latter case, interaction with one's functional group has a higher priority than rapid interaction with other members of the project team. My main point still applies, however: locations should be flexible enough to allow realistic decisions to be made about grouping people according to the priority of their interaction.

From his studies of research organizations, Allen also believes that when work groups are organized according to task interdependence, they will get together even when physically separated; hence, there is greater flexibility, and temporary locations can be chosen on other grounds. My observations support this view, and in Steele (1971) I called the interactions that people will make happen first-order interactions. It is in the second-order interactions – those that are accidental but often very stimulating – that distances take their toll. If there is neither interdependence nor proximity, there is no contact.

Finally, Kleinschrod (1966) suggests that the office-landscape layout developed by the Quickborner team is most efficient under conditions of changing work patterns. It is a system that permits fast and inexpensive changes. One estimate (Anon., 1968) is that the cost of change is 33¢ per square foot versus $5-$10 per square foot in more conventional layout systems. Even more important, a large area can be changed and people regrouped in one afternoon. Both of these features increase the likelihood that an organization will actually change its physical shape as the shape of its tasks changes.

INDIVIDUAL ACTIVITIES

The third type of task activity is that which takes place *inside* the individual; thinking, concentrating, associating, remembering, reading, and so on. Properties of the setting which influence an individual's internal activities include physiological conditions, symbolic properties, interference factors, and sources of stimulation.

Physiological Conditions

The physiological factors of temperature, light, wind, smells, and dampness were discussed earlier. The point was made in the discussion on shelter and security that if these factors are not within certain ranges, that setting is a difficult one in which to do productive work. One can shovel snow quite effectively at 5° below zero, but it is impossible to sit and write in that situation.

Symbolic Properties

Symbolic properties are all aspects of the setting that have meaning for the person using it. Features such as colors, styles of furniture, materials (wood, carpet, etc.), and decorations have message value for people who are using them. These messages tend to trigger associations, memories, feelings, and impressions which in turn influence the thinking about a task. For instance, a friend of mine rearranged his office at a university and was very surprised by the result. Although he cannot say exactly what makes the difference (it could be the fact of change itself), he finds that he concentrates better and enjoys doing creative work in his office more than he did before the rearrangement.

In essence I am talking about the *mood* which a setting evokes in people who are working there. Usually this mood is a function of one's present thoughts and feelings in a place, plus memories of it or similar places from the past. The effect is usually a result of an undefinable mixture of environmental conditions and is very much related to the history and experience of the individual. This was brought home to me very clearly by a Broadway comedy a few years ago about a writer who tried to recreate his mother's kitchen – the scene of his first (and only) successful playwriting venture. He focused on all the details, even down to (purchased) cockroaches, but was unable to recapture the mood. His mood in the earlier scene was more than simply the sum of the individual parts of the setting; it came from a complex relationship between him, the times, and the place.

Interference Factors

Interference factors are those aspects of a setting which allow our concentration to be interrupted without our being able to control the time and nature of the interruption. A feature of open-office design that is often mentioned as detrimental to concentration is the lack of a door. Unless a group develops some other symbol that warns outsiders that they do not want to be disturbed (such as a set of flags), they will have little control over interruptions, and thoughtful work will suffer.

Work spaces that are located in the path of heavy traffic give rise to the same problem. This problem is compounded if the occupants are not protected from the flow by some visual screening, because accidental distractions are quite likely. A colleague told me that he was finally able to concentrate on his work when he moved out of what he called "the fishbowl" – an office that had a glass window looking onto a corridor – into an office with an opaque door. Another manager described his solution to the same problem; he put up a huge bulletin board which blocked visual contacts.

Sources of Stimulation

Sources of stimulation are the opposite of the interference problem. It is possible to be so isolated from contact and visual stimuli that one's ability to be creative runs dry. Creative work generated only by internal sources is usually much less rich than work stimulated by the surroundings as well

Organizations could do a great deal more to promote task creativity if they used more varied settings for different kinds of tasks. For example, a travel agency could work out a large contract in the Roman Colosseum, a football team could watch the films of last week's game on the 50-yard line, a shipping group could meet on a wharf, and railroad executives could hold a meeting in a roundhouse or in the waiting room of a run-down station. The point would be to pick locations for specific meetings that would stimulate creative thinking about the nature of the task and possible solutions to problems.

The shifting of locations seems to happen most naturally in manufacturing and processing operations. When a crisis comes up in the plant, people gather where the trouble is, and they have cues to the solution right there. The problem is that the more removed a work group is from actual physical operations, the more likely the group is to try to be creative in very "flat" environments, such as a conference room, that do not change with the changing nature of the problems.

NORMS ABOUT USE OF SETTINGS

The final influence of settings on task performance cuts across the physical, interaction, and individual categories. This is the influence of group norms which define rules about how a space or setting should be used. Strictly speaking, norms are a property of the social system rather than of the setting, but they combine with the physical properties of the setting to determine what can be done there.

For an example we can take the "clean desk" fad that is followed in many organizations. One manager described this norm about use of settings very clearly:

> We have the clean desk thing here in our executive offices. I have a big desk which is great for spreading out papers, but there is an unwritten rule that your desk should always be clean. Anybody who is a "good" executive is supposed to be totally caught up with all his work and just waiting for the next piece of paper to come sliding across the surface for his approval. It can hurt your career to have stuff spread out, so I take most of the really tough stuff home with me at night and work on it in my study.

In other words, a setting that is adequate for creative problem-solving can be neutralized by a norm about what the efficient executive's desk should look like. The cost to task performance is also magnified by the fact that my friend works on the really tough problems at home, where he cannot have quick discussions with others in his group. It is while working on just those problems that most need testing with others that he is farthest away from them.

My final example is from a consulting team that was having an initial meeting with a client group one evening in the living room of the head of the client group. As one consultant described it:

> The place was arranged like most living rooms are – all right for twos and threes to talk, but not set up for everyone there to see one another easily. We didn't feel that it would be legitimate for us to alter someone's living room, so we tried to operate as best we could. The meeting never got out of the fragmented stage – there was never a time when we were all talking about the same thing as a group. The meeting didn't really serve our purpose, and I don't think it served theirs.

In this case, norms about who can have influence on layout when in someone's personal territory, e.g., his living room, kept the setting from being restructured to fit the task at hand.

8
FUNCTION V: PLEASURE

This dimension is concerned with settings as ends in themselves, that is, the extent to which they provide *pleasure* for the people who are using them. The emphasis is on immediate gratification, rather than on settings as a means to some other end.[1] The measure of this dimension is how people *feel* in a particular setting. Is it a pleasing experience to be there? Do they like being there? Do they feel good while they are there?

While it is true that the physical setting can give us feelings of satisfaction because it meets our needs on other dimensions, such as shelter, social contact, or task accomplishment, it also can serve us as a special end in itself when we get pleasure simply from being in a particular place. This pleasure can take various forms, including feelings of happiness, joy, excitement, wonder, and appreciation of great beauty. Anyone, for instance, who has seen the Painted Desert at sunset no doubt knows what I mean. That setting is a complete end in itself; the setting is its own reward.

I do not mean to imply that only spectacular settings provide immediate gratification, however. For some commonplace examples of

1 I would like to thank Mickey Ritvo for pointing out that I had left this dimension out of my original category system. I was so busy looking at ways the environment helps people do things that I was forgetting that a setting can be enjoyed for its own sake.

how settings can evoke responses of pleasure or displeasure, we can turn to the comments Lynch and Rivkin (1959) recorded while taking subjects for a walk around a block in Boston's Back Bay shopping district. First, a positive response:

> I like the openness, I like the width of the sidewalks, I like the feeling of uncrowded space. You can never feel at the bottom of a well on this spot.

And an example of negative response to a setting:

> This parking lot here has always annoyed me. It separates the shopping. I always hate to walk across the lot from one store to the next.

These quotations are simple examples of what we all know from our own life experiences: there are places we enjoy and will often go out of our way to visit or pass through, and there are places we find distasteful or unpleasant and which we will avoid when we can.

SOURCES OF PLEASURE

There are three major factors that combine to determine whether a setting will be pleasurable for a person. One is the nature of the setting itself – the qualities that give it its definition and character. The other two are related to the person: his past history and his current mood or internal state. The impact of the setting on the pleasure function, moreso than for any of the others discussed in this book, is dependent on the nature of the person using it.

Qualities of the Setting

Qualities of the setting, as indicated earlier, are the source of the sensory stimuli through which a person perceives a place. These stimuli include visual, auditory, olfactory, and tactile experiences produced, respectively, by how a place looks, sounds, smells, and feels.

The number of dimensions on which you can describe the qualities of a setting is endless. Some of the dimensions which we usually consider in thinking about variations in settings are: colors, arrangements of objects, amount and quality of light, smells and sounds, the presence or absence of surprising elements, the look and feel of materials, kinesthetic properties (freedom of movement, confortableness of seating), and the overall characteristics of a place (e.g., well-kept, run-down, natural state, or altered).

When we talk about pleasure from settings, we usually mean whether or not a person finds the particular combination of qualities aesthetically pleasing. After a considerable amount of research to discover particular "rules" about which colors, sounds, and other qualities are most pleasing to people, psychologists have arrived at the conclusion that probably there are no specific "bests" which are good for most people. This is particularly discouraging to industrial psychologists who hoped to provide work organizations with definitive answers as to how their settings should be structured and decorated for maximum enjoyment.

Even though it is not possible to say unequivocally that a particular color will bring pleasure to people, there are some generalizations at a different level of analysis that seem well substantiated. In a summary of work related to the perception of beauty in the environment, Platt (1961) suggests that there are three general properties that are necessary for pleasurable neural functioning: response to stimuli, the pattern of stimuli, and change in stimuli. A lack of stimulation tends to result in boredom, apathy, and if extreme, eventually in hallucinations. Lack of pattern tends to produce feelings of chaos, uncertainty, and anxiety; whereas lack of change in stimuli eventually results in tuning-out and becoming unaware of the setting.

Lynch and Rivkin (1959) illustrate these last two properties in their summary of what people remembered from their walk in the Back Bay shopping area:

> The spaces remembered afterwards seemed to be either those which were clearly defined in form, or which made evident breaks in the general continuity. In certain earlier (and less systematic) interviews for instance, the space of entering cross streets was ignored, except where heavy on-coming traffic forced recognition of the street as a break in continuity. There was a unanimous reaction of dislike to what was described as the "huge and formless" space of a railroad yard.[2]

---

2 K. Lynch and M. Rivkin, "A Walk around the Block," *Landscape*, 8, 1969. Reprinted in Proshansky, *et. al.*, *Environmental Psychology*. New York: Holt, Rinehart & Winston, 1970, p. 638. Reprinted by permission.

As another example of general properties that influence the pleasantness of a setting, compare Figs. 8.1 and 8.2. The first setting would usually be experienced as pleasurable; it has rich stimuli, visual change as the eye scans it, and is organized in a harmony of patterns provided by nature. Most people would find the setting in Fig. 8.2 unpleasant, since it contains a bombardment of stimuli without pattern or recognizable transitions. Furthermore, it probably has the additional drawbacks of loud traffic noise and noxious smells from auto exhausts.

This last example also raises another interesting point about qualities of the setting and the experience of pleasure from it. The absence of noxious (negative, disagreeable, or harmful) stimuli from a setting will tend to make it pleasant, but this alone is not sufficient to provide pleasure. It is not a two-alternative choice, where the opposite of unpleasant is pleasant. There is a third category, that of neutral, or "bland," where the setting contains elements that neither upset us nor please us. Many organizational settings today, unfortunately, fall into this third category; they provide neither positive gratification (pleasure) nor awareness of lost opportunities and the need for change (active displeasure). Thus, these settings add nothing to the lives of those who use them, yet are tolerated and even duplicated when "new" organizational spaces are built.

Finally, the very fact of novelty or change in settings can be a source of satisfaction. In my own situation, a restructuring of my office greatly increased my sense of enjoyment at being in it. The new layout may have been more "beautiful" in some sense, but the most important element to me seemed to be simply the feel of a new place – the fact of change itself. This example speaks for periodic change in one's settings as a way of rekindling waning enjoyment of them.

A Person's History of Past Experiences

A person's past experiences influence the qualities which will stimulate his feelings when he is in a particular setting. At the most general level, growing up in different cultures produces different preferences for art, music, literature, architecture, and so on. Platt (1961) describes how early experiences in a culture create expectations about the structure of things. For example, many Americans are not able to perceive the underlying pattern of a Japanese house, since it violates their culturally determined expectations about what a "house" should be.

Fig. 8.1 A pleasant setting – aspens in New Mexico. (Photography by Ansel Adams. Reprinted from *Sierra Club Bulletin*, October 1970.)

Fig. 8.2 A not-so-pleasant setting. (Photograph by Bruce Anderson.)

The geophysical environment has a conditioning effect similar to that of the social culture. When he asked people to express preferences for pictures of various landscapes, Sonnenfeld (1966) found that people preferred landscapes that were either similar to the geophysical environment of their home or that differed from other choices in ways consistent with their home environment.

At the technophysical environmental level, people are conditioned to like settings that match their previous experiences in particular homes and offices. Parr (1966) reports that people show strong attachments and liking for their early home area, no matter how objectively ugly or run-down it may have been. In a study of preferences for photographs of different types of houses, Michelson (1969) found that people's choices were predictable from a knowledge of the houses in which they had previously lived.

These examples strongly suggest that if it is decided that office spaces will be planned in a new way, i.e., with the participation of the eventual users, it is not enough to just ask them what they want, because they will tend to choose those characteristics they know best from their past. An important step in the process, then, is to generate *new* experiences with features such as open planning that have not been tried before. This should be done not as a means of "selling" another plan, but rather of generating alternatives that the users can realistically consider in their own deliberations.

In his study of a new office building, Manning (1965) found that people liked areas with windows:

> The windows here are marvelous because, before, you were caged in by bars and windows that you couldn't look out of at all. So the windows, lighting, and pleasant surroundings here are a great boon.[3]

In this instance, it seems likely that pleasure with the place comes from its being *different* from a previous setting – specifically, better in terms of the users' perceptions. If there had not been this comparison, the informants would presumably have been less aware of the windows as a direct source of pleasure for them and would have taken them more for granted.

Schachtel (1959) proposes that the childhood training of many people in Western society makes them unable to experience the fullness of immediate pleasure in the present. He notes that children are able to experience a full range of emotions spanning great highs and lows, whereas adults tend to be relatively limited in their ability to be aware of strong and varied feelings related to a particular event. As adults, we have therefore lost something we had in childhood. Schachtel calls this process of loss "childhood amnesia," signifying that we have literally forgotten how to read the full range of our immediate experiences. He hypothesizes

---

3 P. Manning, *op. cit.*, p. 478. Reprinted by permission.

that this amnesia is the result of potent social pressures on us as we grow up. Schools, parents, and friends ask for reports of feelings or thoughts in relatively stereotyped schemata, such as asking us regularly whether we feel good or bad.[4] Over time our emotional vocabulary contracts (rather than expands) as we learn the least complicated ways of satisfying others with accounts of what is happening or has happened to us.

The result is an adult who experiences not the event which is happening to him at a particular moment, but rather the socially prescribed categories which he will use to describe the event to someone later. This process comes between a person and the experiencing of his immediate setting. For example, the ubiquitous camera of the tourist tends to be focused not on the places and people he is photographing but rather on the people to whom he will show the pictures (including himself). This future orientation may greatly reduce the pleasure we get from experiences in our immediate settings.

I believe that each of us suffers to some degree from the blindness to spatial effects that is caused by childhood amnesia. If we expect to create settings that provide more pleasure for their users, we must also, therefore, be concerned about retraining, and reducing the thick shell between a person and his experience that has been built up by his past history.[5]

The Person's Internal State

The third major factor influencing a person's pleasure in his settings is his internal state, i.e., his mood and concerns at a particular time. This mood operates as a filter to provide what Sommer (1969) calls "connotative meaning" to the stimuli that a person receives from his surroundings. For example, I said earlier that most people would get pleasure from being in the woodland scene in Fig. 8.1. However, if a person there were worried about being lost, he would probably get little satisfaction from the natural beauty of the setting. The same features that were pleasing when he was not anxious would be threatening symbols of the vastness of the woods

---

4 Two institutionalized pressures which build up a tendency to see the present only in terms of future description are the "What I did last summer" report and the book report, which encourages continual attention to how a book will be described rather than reading simply for pleasure.

5 The last three chapters of this book, dealing with environmental competence, were written in order to provide some suggestions for actual training exercises and for specific factors on which to work.

the lack of human help, and the possibility of wandering around for a long time. The place is the same, but his internal state has changed.

Similarly, a man who feels good about a meeting he is attending in an elegant old mansion that has been converted to a conference center can get great pleasure from the surroundings, while another participant, who is anxious about his performance at the meeting, may be unaware of the setting or be depressed by it because it reminds him of the elegant life he will probably lose because of his bad performance.

I should note also that there is an interesting circularity to the processes I have just been describing. The setting's impact is affected by the person's internal mood which, in turn, is often influenced by the setting through the memories or fantasies which it triggers off in him. For example, when I am feeling low and go out to walk on certain streets in the Beacon Hill area of Boston, my mood usually begins to improve because of both the beauty of the setting and the memories of pleasurable experiences there in the past. Once my mood begins to change, I see more of what is around me and enjoy the walk still more. I doubt whether the setting alone in an organizational context can neutralize the unpleasurable effects of a really bad social climate, but in more neutral cases the setting can certainly help to tip the balance toward good or bad moods, depending on the structural qualities and personal history discussed above.

PLEASURE FOR WHOM?

In what ways do organizations attempt to deal with the pleasure dimension in environmental design? My observations indicate that aesthetic considerations about organizational settings are most often based on economic criteria, e.g., painting the walls one of three colors that can be bought in volume at a discount; on symbolic grounds, e.g., how the place will look to someone coming in from outside; or on the aesthetic preferences of those in power. For example, it is rumored that in one large organization the president must approve any change that managers and executives make in their own offices, presumably on the assumption that his preferences will be better for them than their own.

Professional designers often collude with top management to make sure that users have little influence over their work place. In 1928, Evelyn Waugh wrote satirically:

> The problem of architecture as I see it . . . is the problem of all art – the elimination of the human element from the consideration of form. The only perfect building must be the factory, because that is built to house machines, not men.[6]

This is a less than perfect stance from the user's standpoint, since the pleasure function of space is the most uniquely "human" of the six functions. Only a person can *feel* something as a result of his surroundings. Machines may function better or worse in different conditions, as shown by the attention paid to climate control for computer installations, but they do not get a kick out of being in one place versus another.

It might be tempting to think that the attitude parodied by Waugh no longer exists, but such is not the case. For instance, a 1970 issue of *Administrative Management* carried an advertisement in which a designer exclaimed "Look what he did to my design!!" "He" was the actual user of an office designed by the man in the advertisement. The user had had the audacity to bring from home a couch that he particularly liked and to put in his office. The point of the advertisement was that the furniture company had a new line of office furniture so complete and interlocking that no user would be able to ruin a fine design by expressing his own preferences.

In general, one is more likely to have pleasurable surroundings as he moves higher in the organization. More is provided for him, and he has more freedom to arrange his own setting. Mogulescu (1970) furnishes an interesting exception to this trend in his design for a client company:

> It is the service department employees who most require an outside view and the convenience of working under direct daylight conditions as a means of alleviating monotony.[7]

His solution was to put clerical, technical, and secretarial employees on the windowed outside perimeter and executives on the inside core – a design that goes against traditional symbolic locations in most organizations. This is not quite the break with tradition that it might seem, however, since further on he notes that two-foot clerestories (vertical skylights set in the interior walls) were installed in the interior sections to let in as much light as possible, a refinement that is usually dispensed with when lower-level

---

6 E. Waugh, *Decline and Fall.* 1928 (Penguin edition, 1937), p. 120.

7 M. Mogulescu, *op. cit.*, p. 106. Reprinted by permission.

employees are on the inside. The symbolic language is still there – in the amount of extra effort taken on the inside offices – but at least the lower-level employees have a nicer setting than usual.

ORGANIZATIONAL CONSEQUENCES

As I pointed out at the beginning of this chapter, the focus of the pleasure function of settings is on pleasure as an end in itself. Individual satisfaction has therefore been the main focus of my discussion, but that does not mean that there are no implications for social system functioning. In closing this chapter I will touch briefly upon such implications.

One generalization can be made from the notion of pleasure itself. If people experience pleasure in a place, they are more likely to also experience satisfaction with being there. There is, in fact, some research evidence to support this assumption. In a comparison of interviews done in "ugly" (drab, sparse metal furniture) and "beautiful" (comfortable furniture, warm colors) rooms, Maslow and Mintz (1956) found that the interviews finished more quickly in the ugly rooms. Since neither the subject nor the interviewer knew the real purpose of the study, their conclusion was that the unpleasant surroundings encouraged those in the ugly rooms to finish their task and get out quickly.

Most large organizations have acres of offices at least as drab as the ugly room in the Maslow and Mintz study. They also have many settings which are experienced as unpleasant because of crowding or lack of control over one's personal space. From this discussion we can assume that when people have a choice, (a) they will tend not to go to those kinds of settings, (b) they will hurry to finish what they are doing there so they can leave as soon as possible, or (c) they will psychologically block out their displeasure and dissatisfaction with the setting, thus reducing their awareness of how they feel. The costs to the person are stress, dissipated energy, and dissatisfaction. The costs to the system are reduced contact (people see one another less frequently if they stay away from the work setting), hurriedly completed tasks, and emotionally limited human beings.

These emotional costs also suggest that the settings have an effect on the values people place on themselves and the institution. I believe that when someone uses a setting that he enjoys and feels good about, he tends to feel better about himself and his organization than if he operates in a setting that he does not like.

This effect often shows up clearly when people move from an unpleasant to a pleasant setting, or vice versa. Manning describes this process in his study of a new office building:

> It is interesting to note that the standard of care taken by employees in the toilets has improved out of all recognition. A 5 PM inspection of all male and female toilets showed them to be immaculate; this was certainly not the experience in the old buildings. It seems, therefore, that the provision of high amenity levels has resulted in much better behaviour and treatment of the property.[8]

My interpretation goes slightly beyond Manning's; I see the employees' new behavior directed at the "property" as a means of expressing feelings toward both themselves (who have to use the toilets) and the institution (which provides and owns the toilets). Their behavior says to me that they are feeling better about both.

---

8 P. Manning, *op. cit.*, p. 479. Reprinted by permission.

9
FUNCTION VI: GROWTH

The last major function of physical settings is to promote *growth* in the people who use them. By growth I mean any of a number of developmental processes: learning new skills; achieving a greater sense of self-esteem; becoming more aware of one's personal preferences, style, strengths, and weaknesses; achieving a greater sense of competence in dealing with the world; or understanding more about how the world around one functions (including relevant social systems). Settings also have an impact on group growth, particularly in the areas of group norms and group problem-solving ability. The central question for this section is whether the setting facilitates the user's development of his potential abilities and personal qualities.

There are two primary avenues to the growth of personal potential: (1) A person perceives some new pattern or element which he then incorporates into an expanded view or understanding of his world. The new pattern can be external or internal (e.g., a feeling) to himself; (2) A person (a) perceives a problem, (b) chooses some course of action to deal with the problem, (c) takes action, (d) receives feedback about the effectiveness of his action, and (e) incorporates this feedback into a view of his own competence in purposefully affecting his environment.

In this chapter I will describe two main factors in settings which influence these growth processes. One is the setting's physical qualities, which affect perception and the opportunity for action. The other is the setting's effect on social interaction, which in turn affects the amount of support for the growth process.

PHYSICAL QUALITIES

There are many characteristics of environmental settings that help determine whether a person will be stimulated toward growth. The ones that I have chosen for illustration here are diversity, visibility, changeability, and demand.

Diversity of Stimulation

The greater the number and intensity of stimuli in a setting, the more likely that setting is to trigger new perceptions, new thoughts and feelings, and new connections between previously unconnected elements. Studies on sensory deprivation with adults have indicated that over time a dull, monotonous environment tends to promote a person's withdrawal into himself, a blocking of experimentation, and a sense of lack of control over his environment (Fiske, 1961).

The effect of diversity on child development is even more pronounced. As Parr (1969) points out, small children are restricted in mobility compared with adults, and in order to develop they need the "sensory rewards of exploration that only a fine-grained diversity can provide." By "fine-grained," he means a high degree of detail within a relatively limited area. For example, a century-old wood-paneled wall seen at a distance appears fairly uniform, but a closer look reveals new patterns and details in the wood. By contrast, a perfectly white plaster wall reveals little new detail upon closer examination.

The primary focus of Parr's observation is really on mobility. The more a worker's movements are restricted to a small area, the more his growth depends on a diversity of stimulation in his immediate surroundings.

A place promotes growth not only through the amount of stimulation, but also through the *patterns* of stimuli, particularly if the patterns are unexpected or novel. Unexpected arrangements help to break old habits of seeing or behaving. For example, Smith (1969) describes a recent practice of some Italian architects who exhibit Renaissance paintings on steel I-beams or wood scaffolds:

> The contrasting machine age easel produces an immediate alienation effect that tends to refocus our vision on the actual painting rather than its venerable age.[1]

The more surprising the physical features of a setting are, the more likely we are to respond nonautomatically and with an experimental attitude.

Visibility

A physical setting that allows people to *see* how things work is more likely to promote growth, especially in understanding that setting and the person's opportunities to use it.

I have referred throughout the book to my house designed by David Sellers at Prickley Mountain in Vermont. One of our central goals there has been to create a setting for living and working that would be growth-producing. In the evolution of the house, visibility emerged as one of the most important factors facilitating this growth. The house is built with joining systems, wiring conduits, and other structural features exposed to view and organized in aesthetically pleasing configurations (see Fig. 9.1). This contrasts with the vast majority of buildings in this country, where it is assumed that working features of the house, such as the wiring, should be hidden behind cosmetic wall surfaces. My feeling is that if the real life processes of a house are hidden, the house is dead in terms of what the user can learn there.

Visibility and growth are connected in much larger systems than houses. Carr and Lynch (1968) suggest that the more observable the processes and structures of a city are to its residents, the more likely they are to learn about the city and themselves. For example, I believe that the New York City subway system is so disorganized visually (compared, for instance, with the London Underground) that it is possible to use it for a long time without really learning very much about it or the overall transportation system of the city.

Changeability

Changeability is the extent to which a physical setting can be easily and quickly altered. Movable furniture, changeable wall locations, drapes that

---

1 C.R. Smith, "The Great Museum Debate," *Progressive Architecture*, December 1969, p. 82.

Fig. 9.1 Exposed conduits and building system in Steele House at Prickley Mountain. (Photograph by Joel Katz/*Yale Alumni Bulletin*.)

change light and visibility characteristics of a place, materials that can be marked or attached-to without damage help to provide a manipulable setting where people can take action to change a place and get feedback as to whether their choices were effective for what they were trying to do.

Here is a fine example of a dormitory designed with the changeability factor in mind, a new building at Pembroke College:

> The suites, with three or four rooms each, allow for differentiation in use by the students living in them. All rooms can be used as combined bedroom-study rooms, or students may cluster their study, sleeping, or social activities by sharing spaces. Rooms have been kept simple in configuration so that variations in patterns of use and furniture arrangement will have a discernable impact on the character of the rooms and allow students further opportunity to affect their immediate environment. . . The solution is the antithesis of Eero Saarinen's Morse and Stiles Colleges at Yale, to which, alas, nothing can be added (or subtracted), and is, therefore, inorganic.[2]

At Morse and Stiles Colleges, furniture is fully designed and built into place, and the space tolerances are so small that almost no new furniture can be added. The Pembroke setting promotes growth through its manipulability, whereas the Yale buildings may have been a growth experience for the designers, but are not likely to be one for the students.

It is my impression that the trends in office layout and furniture design are more in the Yale spirit. One exception is the Herman Miller Organization's "Action Office II," a system of components (desk, chairs, table top, lighting sources, etc.) that can be organized by the user according to his own work style. The user who experiments with this system is very likely to learn about his own work style and about new possibilities.

Unfortunately, flexibility in the setting is not a *guarantee* of growth; it just makes it more likely. In order for new patterns to emerge, a person must *use* the flexibility available to him. One space-planning firm reported to me that their clients varied widely in the degree to which they explored the potential of Action Office II. Those who do not care to experiment set up Action Office II to resemble their last office and then leave it unchanged. The result is another example of pseudo-fixed-feature space.

Finally, it is my observation that the vast majority of houses in this country have relatively few areas of easy changeability. I believe that this built-in rigidity accounts in part for the middle-class housewife's emphasis

---

2 "First Design Award," *Progressive Architecture*, January 1970, pp. 133-134. Reprinted by permission.

on cleaning. Cleaning is one of the few opportunities she has to create a visible difference in a house where the walls are fixed, and the walls, floors, furniture, etc., are not to be marked or changed. Unfortunately, this manipulation is repetitive and only gets her back to where she was before the house got dirty. Few new ideas or patterns emerge from this process, so there is little likelihood that the cleaner will perceive things in new ways or that her self-esteem will be raised through the effects of her own choices. Furniture does get shifted from time to time, but the function of specific rooms usually does not change.

Demand Quality

Demand quality is the extent to which the setting *requires* that something be done to it – that some choices be made and action taken on them – in order for the setting to be used. An incomplete or inappropriate setting is more likely to promote growth in its users than a structured setting that people can "get by" with.

For an example of this quality in a setting, consider Kohl's (1969) description of a teacher thinking about how to begin the new school year:

> Why not leave the room just as it is [the chairs have been piled upon the tables and pushed into a corner] and see what happens when the students enter? He had other plans, ones carefully nurtured over the summer. He would set up the tables in small groups and let the children sit where they chose . . . But the idea of leaving things as they are may be a better way to begin the year. Perhaps it might be possible to make organization of the class a collaborative venture between him and his students, and among the students themselves.[3]

In this instance, I am glad that the teacher followed his intuitions. By dealing with an unarranged room, the students would be more likely to learn something about who they were, who the teacher was, and what they were trying to do in that classroom than if the classroom were set up according to the teacher's plan. Of course, learning could take place in the latter setting, but the physical setting itself would not contribute much to the growth process.

Old houses and buildings used as offices often have this demand quality. They must be "worked on" to be habitable, and this often leads

3 H. Kohl, "Teaching the Unteachable," Reprinted with permission from *The New York Review of Books*. Copyright © 1967 Herbert Kohl.

to a heightened sense of *esprit de corps* in the group as well as a heightened awareness of space by individuals. Sometimes this becomes clearer when a group moves into "improved" quarters – a new office building in which the people should feel good, but where they in fact feel less alive than they did in the older place.

Settings do not have to be old and run down, however, in order to have a demand quality. A colleague recently described to me a new research laboratory whose design he had influenced. Basically, it is one large space with various zones defined within the space: a bench area for experiments, a file area for information storage, a desk zone for writing and spreading out papers, meeting spaces where several people can get together, and a reading area with journals, books, good light, and comfortable seats. The key feature is that there are no permanently assigned offices or desks that are used exclusively by a single person. Instead, the researchers shift to different zones as their activities change.

When these plans were first developed, the users doubted that they could really function properly without having permanent work places available. Preliminary interviews indicate, however, that having worked within this setup for some time, they are excited by the arrangement and would not change back to the old pattern. In our terms, the setting has high demand quality; people must be specific about what activity they are about to begin and which kind of zone is most appropriate for that activity. My prediction is that this will develop greater awareness of their work styles, increase understanding of the ways in which activities and places do or do not fit together, and generally enhance their existential awareness of their work world. Thus, a high demand setting does not have to be old; it just has to require choice and action by the users in order for it to be complete.

Demand quality promotes the growth of groups as well as individuals. In the example above from Kohl, the *class,* not just the individual students, developed from dealing with the furniture. Similarly, Duhl (1968) describes a case where a physical setting issue which required action (the location of a new medical center) served as the vehicle for development of a community's competence at problem-solving and group action. In his view (and mine) the growth of the community was more important in the long run than the physical issue which triggered the problem.

I believe that the physical setting is a particularly good medium for the development of group problem-solving abilities, because the setting is concrete, immediate, and visible. When action is taken, people can see and feel the difference it makes, whereas actions taken on fuzzier social system issues most often lead to changed attitudes and opinions that are not readily observable. In order for the concreteness of settings to be used for growth of group competence, however, there must be a minimum level of openness in the group which allows them to talk about what they did and the effects of their action.

SOCIAL INTERACTION

Through their effect on social interaction settings also promote the growth of individuals or groups. Characteristics of settings that affect this process include the amount of contact the setting allows, the visibility of people to one another, and the messages the setting sends about possible new patterns of contact.

Amount of Contact

As I discussed in the chapter on social contact, settings tend to either promote or block personal interaction. As a result, they do have an effect on the degree to which people will satisfy these social needs, as well as an impact on individual growth and change. For example, the trend toward high-security apartment "enclaves" that I described in the chapter on shelter and security exacts a high cost by stifling growth. As groups build up walls that separate them from people unlike themselves (who may be "the enemy"), they also lose the opportunity to experience and examine the real differences between themselves and those they have locked out. The more a particular group, such as middle-class whites or militant blacks, segregates itself from those who are different, the less likely the group is to have its views of the world challenged or modified. The resulting stagnation and lack of growth are basically antihuman. Kahlil Gibran sensed this in the protective, fortress-like houses built close together in his native Lebanon:

> In their fear your forefathers gathered you too near together. Would that I could gather your houses into my hand, and like the sower scatter them in the forest and meadow.[4]

---

4 W. Ellis, "Lebanon: Little Bible Land in the Crossfire of History," *National Geographic*, 137, 2, February 1970, pp. 258-259.

Similarly, many office layouts encourage a particular group to interact with its own members and discourage others from entering. The more a group feels threatened by the rest of the system, the more likely it is to structure its spaces to keep others out by using signs, unmarked entrances, and a gauntlet of challenging secretaries who are called *receptionists* but would be more aptly titled *rejectionists*. These arrangements may promote a sense of internal security in the group, but they reduce contacts with the outside and consequently erect barriers that keep out fresh thought and foster a nongrowth, in-bred environment. There are fewer external checks on the group's collective view of the world than if the setting invited contacts between the group and nonmembers.

Visibility

As with physical systems, the visibility of social systems tends to promote the growth of their members. One advantage of the trend toward open-office layouts without full-height walls is that people can *see* the organization at work, can sense the centers of activity and the flow of work, and can get a better sense for the system as a whole and where they fit into it. In a comparison of two community development laboratories (Steele, 1968), I found a similar phenomenon. The community grew more organized and connected in a campus-type setting, which allowed people to see comings and goings, than it did in a high-rise setting where almost no part of the place was visible from any other part.

There is, however, one area in which visibility may inhibit growth rather than enhance it, namely, that of control and authority relations. A person may resist a change of location that would make him more visible to his boss or to other superiors in the hierarchy. This resistance is explained partly by a need for autonomy which, among other things, allows a person to make his own mistakes and learn from them. The clearest example I have found of visibility-authority relations is the following:

> A company had been having great difficulty in one particular section in getting subordinates to take any initiative in their work. A physical change finally got them started. Their supervisors, who used to sit at desks adjacent to them in an open office, were moved to another location. The bosses could therefore no longer listen to phone conversations, send hand signals, and generally second-guess their subordinates. The subordinates began to make more decisions and

> take more risks, since their bosses were just not around so much. The subordinates also began to get feedback about *their* choices, rather than simply about their bosses' decisions.

Similar situations exist in many organizations; that is, visibility must be reduced in order to promote the growth of subordinates.

Messages About New Possibilities

Finally, settings facilitate growth through the symbolic messages they provide users about possible new ways of relating to one another. For instance, the layout of a new open office often suggests to its inhabitants that maybe they can be overheard without the disastrous consequences they had fantasized about in the past. If they then experiment with freer discussion and the sky does not fall in, they have learned that they can be a little freer with one another.

Another example I encountered recently is considerably more extreme than that of the open office. During a weekend conference, someone hung "his" and "hers" signs on opposite doors to the only bathroom. The room was eventually used simultaneously by men and women – an experiment which was both useful, given the limited facilities, and growth-producing, since the members of the conference expanded their views of whether or not it was essential to maintain absolute privacy between the sexes. The setting played the major part in this experimentation, both because there was only one room and because the signs forced people to ask "why not" about simultaneous use rather than to ask "why."

GROWTH SETTINGS AND INDIVIDUAL DIFFERENCES

There is an important final point which concerns both the physical and social impact of space on the growth process. It has sometimes been called the "U-curve Hypothesis" (e.g., Schroder, Driver, and Streufert, 1968). The notion is that growth occurs when a person is stimulated within a given range of intensity. Conversely, growth is blocked when stimulation is either too low to have any effect or so great that it becomes overwhelming and the person becomes threatened and withdraws. Thus, for both persons and groups, there should be optimal ranges of changeability, unexpectedness, social contact, demands for change, and so on.

This suggests that the question of whether a setting will stimulate growth cannot be answered until one specifies whose growth. What one person finds to be useful stimulation, another will experience as such a threat that he merely shuts it out. This may have happened to a number of people in the bathroom example cited, or in open-office layouts where some people are so threatened by lack of privacy that they never dare to test the consequences of being overheard. Therefore, the question of how much stimulation is useful for any given individual is in practice answerable only by reference to the particular person or group; what one person finds to be an overload, someone else may learn a great deal from.

Similarly, since growth is a process measured against the starting point, settings have to be reassessed periodically to see whether their growth stimulation potential is still the same as before. A setting that requires members of a group to do new problem-solving may become routine after they have mastered it, and that setting will no longer be a factor in their growth, although it could be for someone else. To ensure growth, it is therefore particularly important to be fully aware of the characteristics and the developmental history of individuals or groups for which a stimulating setting is to be designed.

10
THE FUNCTIONS IN PRACTICE

In this chapter I will describe different aspects of the use of the six-functions system and provide some examples of the ways in which it has been employed to facilitate organizational change. I shall briefly mention interconnections among the functions, examples of ratings for different situations, methods for data collection in arriving at ratings, and provide a summary of the uses of the system which are relevant for the consultant who uses physical settings as a medium in his change efforts.

INTERCONNECTIONS AMONG THE FUNCTIONS

The six functions of the spatial environment are, in real life, not nearly so discrete as described here. For instance, a setting often promotes one function because it affects another function positively. The following are some examples. A setting that provides *pleasure* also enhances *task* output if performance is related to the workers' being in good spirits and having high morale. A setting that provides *pleasure* may also promote *social contact* because it draws more people to it more of the time than would a nonpleasurable one. A setting that facilitates *social contact* will often also stimulate *growth* because it makes people see similarities and differences in one another.

In some instances settings are negative on one or more dimensions while being positive on others. In the *social contact* example above, the setting will be negative on *growth* if contact is encouraged only between people who are very much alike, as in segregated facilities in racially intolerant areas. Similarly, a house that rates high on *security* and *pleasure* can be so comfortable that it stimulates no problem-solving or experimentation, and thus is low on *growth*.

Finally, it is not necessary that a setting be given a rating on all six dimensions. For instance, a setting may be positive on two of the dimensions, negative on two, and essentially neutral on two. If there are no tasks being done in a place, then *task* aspects of the place are neutral. Similarly, many places tend to be neutral on *growth*, neither promoting it nor inhibiting it.

THE RATING PROCESS

In diagnoses the categories are used as follows. First, I select a place to rate, usually because a client has asked me to comment on it, but sometimes because my own observations suggest that it is an important area for the client's functioning. I then select particular elements within the place that are likely to influence the functioning of individuals or groups in the client system. Each element may be a particular *thing*, such as a wall, a desk, a lighting arrangement, the color of a particular machine, and so on. It may be the pattern of a *set* of elements, such as an arrangement of chairs, the relative location of offices to one another, etc. Or it may be a *sociological* factor, such as a set of norms about who can use the snack bar.

After choosing each element, I give it a rough rating on the six functions. I have most often used a simple, three-point scale: positive, neutral, and negative (+, 0, –), although I have also used a scale ranging from +3 to –3.

For each of the functions, I ask questions guided roughly by the considerations described in Chapters 4 through 9. To summarize very briefly:

> *Security and Shelter*: Does the element provide protection from physical and psychological stresses? Is it possible for users to withdraw when necessary, and does this element help, hinder, or not affect that process?

Social Contact: Does the element promote, inhibit, or not relate to social contact; and for whom? Does it structure relative locations, control mobility, send signals about who ought to be interacting, and so on?

Symbolic Identification: What messages does the element send about the owners or users and what image they want? What information is there about the system, persons in the system, and individuals? (Note that this scale ranges from high information content to low or zero, not positive to negative.)

Task Instrumentality: What tasks are being done here and how does the element help or hinder in physical tasks, interactional tasks, and internal (concentration) tasks?

Pleasure: To what extent does the element provide pleasure for those who are using it? What are the visual, auditory, olfactory, and tactile stimuli that influence a person's enjoyment? What messages does the place send that may trigger memories of past experiences that a user brings with him to the place?

Growth: To what extent does the element promote growth for the specific people who use it? What is the degree of diversity, problem-solving demand, surprise, and visible feedback about results of action? How much does the place stimulate growth-producing contacts?

Three points should be emphasized. First, it is important to be specific. Any single item or combination can be rated as long as we are specific about what it is we are rating. For instance, we can rate a particular office chair on pleasure. We can also rate the pattern of sameness of all chairs in a department. The former could be positive on *pleasure* whereas the latter pattern is negative, although providing *symbolic* information about uniformity in the department. Second, we must be specific about the person or group *for whom* the rating is given. A particular office-entrance arrangement may be positive on *security* for people who use it every day and negative for first-time visitors, whom it makes uncomfortable. Third, a rating may be different for the same person at different times.

SOURCES OF DATA FOR RATINGS

The most important information I can provide here is an explanation of what data I use to make the ratings for the different functions. In part, my ratings result from practice and an intuitive process developed over time and through my interest in behavior in physical settings. But there are also more concrete sources of data which I use, and the intuitive part probably plays its biggest role in determining how well I use them. These sources include observations, interviews, touring interviews, and change events.

Observations

Observations are a prime source of data for my ratings of work settings. I move around and try to get an overall "feel" for the place, including my own responses to it. Also very helpful are patterns of use which I observe: where people go freely and where they do not go, who has first call on certain facilities and who has no call at all, the symbolic messages that I receive as I look around, the extent to which flexibility in a place is being used or not, where people choose to be when they have real choice, and who can get together easily and who cannot. For all of these, I try to be as aware as I can of elements, patterns of elements, and their effects on the users.

Interviews

Interviews with users are essential to sound ratings, since my reactions to a place may differ from those of the people who have to use it all the time or whose experiences differ from mine. I try always to talk with a number of people who have been using a place, to get their feelings about how good its elements are for social contact, tasks, and so on. It is especially important to get user reactions on the security, growth, and pleasure dimensions, since they depend so much on the state of the individual user. The users also can "clue you in" to symbolic messages that you would not pick up, not knowing the spatial language of the particular organization or group. At times I have encountered resistance from top management to my efforts at interviewing the people who actually use a place. One can be tempted, like higher management, to think that he already knows what effects a place has on people, but there is no substitute for cross checking his impressions with the people involved, just as in gathering observational data there is no substitute for getting out and moving around the organization.

The Touring Interview

The touring interview is really a combination of observations and interviews. I ask a client to walk around his spaces with me and free-associate about what he sees and feels. I also ask specific questions from time to time, if he has not mentioned an element that I think is significant. However, I try to wait until the client has mentioned whatever is relevant to him, since I do not want my own set of significant elements fed back to me. The aim is to get inside the world of the user. I should add that the touring interview can be used with very different environmental scales. In fact, the idea was suggested to me by Lynch and Rivkin's (1959) "walk around the block" technique for studying how a city area affects people. The tour process can be used for a city, a building, a floor, a shopping area, or even one office.

"Change" Events

Change events are another source of data about the impact a setting is having on its users. For instance, the degree of emotionality with which people respond to a move to new quarters can tell us a great deal about how they have been using their setting symbolically and in other ways. The girl I mentioned earlier who was moved to a dead-end hallway discovered through the change how beneficial her former location had been for social contact. Similarly, the blossoming forth of the subordinates whose bosses had been moved to distant offices was indicative of how growth had been stifled by the previous layout. In another company with which I was working, the jockeying by several executives to have a new vice-president in an office adjacent to them revealed how they were using visibility to control and check up on one another. All of these examples fit the old dictum that the quickest way to understand the function of something is to try to change it.

KEEPING TRACK OF THE RATINGS

Clearly, the category system of functions of space we have developed so far is not a tight set of rating scales. The six dimensions are not scales at all, in one sense, since they suggest quantity only in very rough measure. The main purpose of the system is not to produce numerical results that are reliable, but rather to provide a set of focusing lenses through which the various functions of a setting can be sorted out and seen more clearly.

To this end, I have found it helpful to use a simple coding sheet which allows me to make entries for each function and see these entries side by side for a given element. I have reproduced the form in Fig. 10.1, complete with ratings given for an airport waiting lounge. A few explanatory comments should help in understanding how the form is used.

First, (*m*) indicates that the inference is from my own observation, (*u*) that it is from a user's report (in the airport, I interviewed several people while I was waiting for a plane). There may be conflicting responses in a cell, between either (*m*) and (*u*) or among different (*u*) entries.

Second, I try to provide as much qualitative content as possible, going well beyond a simple +, 0, or – rating. This is essential on the symbolic function in order to determine what messages the element provides and to whom. Note that for each dimension I try to be explicit about the item being rated and on whom it is having the effect.

Finally, a little practice actually rating places helps a great deal. I would encourage the reader to try it. All he needs is energy, paper and pencil, eyes, and a willingness to talk to people. One of the advantages of studying the physical setting is that we are always in one, so we always have data for practice.

SOME EXAMPLES OF RATINGS

Perhaps the clearest means of providing a feel for how the ratings work is to describe briefly a few organizational situations and the ratings they received when I used the categories. In some of the situations the functions are working together, and in some they are in conflict with one another.

–A personnel director was becoming more and more of a resource for general organization development activities. Many employees also used him as counselor and confidant. When he was promoted to Senior Vice-President in recognition of his abilities, he was told that henceforth his secretary would work inside his office, which was the organization's cue as to who was a *senior* vice-president. He found it hard to hold the spontaneous meetings he had held in his office before, because of typewriter noise. He also found that people confided in him less because of the extra set of ears that were always present in the office.

In this instance, a setting change forced upon the man by the organization for purposes of *symbolic identification* negatively affected the *task*

Place *Airport waiting lounge* Date *Nov 7, 1970*

	Function*					
Element or pattern	*S/S*	*So*	*Sy*	*T*	*P*	*G*
Linoleum floor (grey)	(M,U):(−) cold, drafty glare	(M):(−) with fixed chairs, reduces contact, can't sit on floor.	cold, efficient, clean, unfriendly, says it's a business area.	O	(M,U):(−) ugly, glare, color is wearing	O
Plastic chairs around periphery of space; none in the center, bolted down.	slightly(−)—hard after long use.	(U):(−) people can't talk. One group said they were split up by it.	impermanence; mass movement (like cattle)	(M):(−) for business chats, only 3 at the most can hear each other.	(M,U):(−) we all thought they were ugly, and not comfortable.	(M):(−) no movement or experimenting possible
Flourescent lights—fairly intense.	(M,U):(+) no eye strain.	(M): (slight −) no intimacy possible in that light.	cold, harsh, says there is nobody's personality here.	(M,U):(+) good for reading.	(M):(−) I don't like the look of it. Feel the glare (with floor)	O
Windows on one side looking out on an airfield.	(U):(−) for those sitting under them drafty; (O for others)	(U): (slight −) as people stared out windows (for those facing w)	Shows what the place is about—air travel	O	(U):(+) for those facing. O for those not	O (or slight + for those facing)
Location of lounge—at far end of corridor, away from all counters	(U):(slight −) away from bathrooms.	(M):(−) no contact with other travelers. (+) increases contact with same flite	Says that this flite is slightly "out of it"—not regular schedule.	(M):(−) for agents and staff—don't get down here much to help passengers.	O	(M):(slight +) pass through many airport areas to get here.
One narrow entrance to waiting area, past check-in counter.	O (except (−) if fire started	(M):(−) people seeing others off slightly intimidated.	Clear message about where to go—no ambiguity.	(M,U):(+) for agent. can control the crowd from one spot.	O	O
Temperature about 60° in the lounge	(M,U):(−) several people complained, felt stiff.	O	Don't know; may be that this is a transition zone—neither inside nor out.	(M):(+) for agents: people don't fall asleep. Keep moving. (−) for reading	(M,U):(−) doesn't feel good or homey (!)	(M):(−) people keep coats on, see little of one another learn nothing new.

Summary: *Not bad for its purpose. Good design for the agents, not so good for travelers. Hard to talk, or sit for long; good for reading till you get cold. Probably easy to clean, but unpleasant because of it. A transition area, not a place of its own, really.*

(M) = my own observation; (U) = data from other users.
* Symbols: S/S = Shelter & Security; So = Social Contact; Sy = Symbolic Identification; T = Task; P = Pleasure; G = Growth

Fig. 10.1 A functions of space coding sheet.

function. He had to put more energy into finding a meeting room (or trying to find another place). He also received less information about the climate of opinion in the organization. *Social contact* increased between him and his secretary, but, decreased between him and those who now came to see him less frequently, and he reported feeling estranged from people whom he cared about. *Pleasure* was also reduced for both him and his secretary, since they felt as though they were always under each other's eye. In this respect, psychological *shelter* was also reduced.

– When people decorate their home or office to a point where they think they have it "right," they will often hesitate to change things around, even if their needs change or they just have an urge to experiment.

This feeling of fixedness in a setting tends to have a negative effect on both *growth* and *pleasure* for those who enjoy tinkering with their settings. The function coming into play is *symbolic identification*: the person thinks his place is sending the "correct" message to others. There may also be a positive element on *security* and *shelter* here. From what we know, *task* and *social contact* would have to be considered neutral in this situation.

– A group of young lawyers working for indigent clients moved into an office building that had cubicles for private offices around the outside perimeter of the space and a large area in the middle which the building's owner described as "the secretarial area." Rather than accept this version of how they should work, they put their secretaries in the private offices and themselves out in the open area.

In this case the locations were chosen for *task* reasons: the lawyers needed to consult one another frequently, and they found this very easy to do in the open area. Typewriter noise was also controlled by having the secretaries in the private offices. The lawyers were willing to give up the traditional *symbolic identification* of "more important = more privacy." *Social contact* as an end in itself was also increased for the lawyers, who said that in previous jobs they had felt more distant emotionally from colleagues than under the new arrangement. However, *social contact* was now negative for the secretaries; they could not talk and relax with one another while at their desks, as they had been able to do previously.

RATINGS AND VALUES

Most of the emphasis until now has been on using the six-functions system to clarify the effects of particular settings and their elements. I have emphasized this process because in my experience it has been the one most often skipped when people try to improve their settings. They usually come up with a judgment – a place is good or bad, or it should look like this or that – before they have examined the existing setting to get a clear picture of what it actually provides for them. The six functions are designed to help people look at what *is* before they skip to what *should* be, to make trade-offs more visible, and to move beyond simplistic rules about what "good" and "bad" spaces are like.

With this in mind, I want to emphasize one point: a place's rating on the six dimensions does *not* automatically indicate whether it is good or bad for the users. It merely discloses what the place provides or blocks for them. Whether this is good or bad depends on what the users *want* or what is necessary for the system to survive. Thus, a positive rating on social contact for office layout says only that interaction is made easy. Whether this is good or bad depends on one's view of the effects of this contact. Similarly, a home very highly positive on security and safety may not be really beneficial to the user, because these very features stifle growth, a process he needs for survival. My choice of terms for the ratings may seem somewhat confusing, but I hope that my intention is clear. When I rate a function as positive, neutral, or negative, I make a purely quantitative statement that does not include the particular value the function may have to a given user, although his and my ratings may be correlated positively. A related point is that the usefulness of a place to a person should be judged by looking at the pattern of ratings on all *six* dimensions, since there are usually trade-offs.

USE OF THE SOCIOPHYSICAL APPROACH FOR CHANGE

Given these qualifications, we can see that the ratings are not an end in themselves. They provide a means for developing a view of what exists and suggesting the directions that new alternatives might take. It is still up to the consultant, designer, or organization member to apply this view to a concrete process of change. I believe that there are many different ways in which a sociophysical view of the world can help the processes of individual and organizational change. In the remainder of this chapter I will discuss several key uses for this outlook.

1. *Changing an Organization's Spaces to Provide a Better Setting for the Users.* The aim of this process is to improve a setting so that it is better

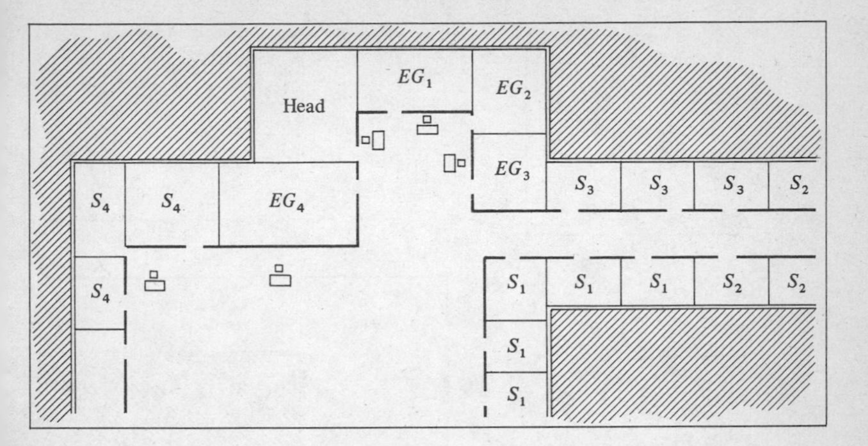

Fig. 10.2 The initial plan (EG = executive group member; S_1 = subordinate of EG_1, etc.).

for the health of the system and its members. The six functions help diagnose what the present settings are providing, and thereby suggest ways in which they can be improved.

Here is a case example from my own work:

> A company asked me to consult with them about changes in their physical layout. They were about to remodel their offices, and they wanted to take advantage of that opportunity to do some real restructuring, not just face-lifting. In particular, they wanted to develop a sense of identity and rapport among the top members reporting to the head of the organization. They were aware that the way the executives were interspersed with their subordinates made interaction difficult. At the same time, they were also alert to the dangers of creating an "executive row" that excluded all other levels, and the executives wanted to maintain contact with their subordinates as well as with their peer group.
>
> In spite of this awareness, they had arrived at a tentative layout that looked like that in Fig. 10.2 – an executive suite layout that would not only intimidate many of the lower-echelon employees, but would increase the distance between most executives and their subordinates.

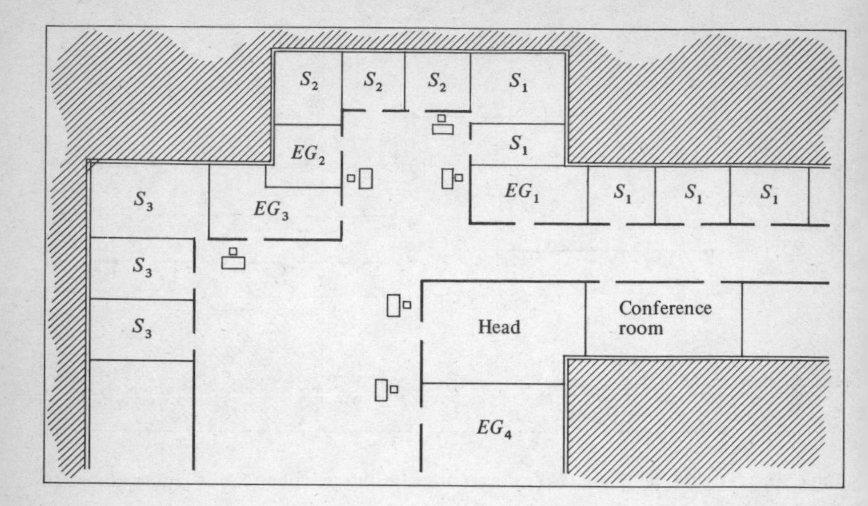

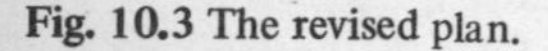
Fig. 10.3 The revised plan.

As we talked about why this particular scheme had been chosen, the main reason given was that the head of the company wanted his executives near him and near one another. As we talked, however, it became clearer that this particular means of achieving those ends had been dictated by some other factors, namely, that the area being used had always been high-status. It had two corners, larger offices, and more windows, all of which made the group assume that only executives could use that space. The symbolic assumptions were really most potent here, although on a somewhat unconscious level.

After I described the assumptions as I saw them and the conflicts between their symbolic assumptions and their stated task and social contact goals, we worked out another layout which traded off some of the symbolic functions. This is shown in Fig. 10.3 and is basically a pinwheel with the head of the organization at the center, the executive group around him, and the subordinates fanning out from each boss. Groups that needed more day-to-day functional contact were placed on adjacent "spokes" of the wheel.

Clarifying what they were giving up on the task and social dimensions in their first scheme helped the group decide that this loss was too high a price to pay for the symbolic use of the corner for the head.

They also broke through their assumption that offices had to be the same size, but they were able to keep some of their status language intact by maintaining appropriate differentials. Even in this respect they became less rigid and put several people in offices larger than they "deserved," in order to facilitate contact. Before our diagnostic session they had assumed that there were no real choices available because the building was old with fixed interior corridor walls; as long as they stuck to their assumption that the president had to be in the corner office, they were right. When they dropped that assumption, they opened up many new alternatives. Note that they also added a conference room which, among other things, would be used in management training and would give the trainees access to what otherwise could seem like a taboo area.

Of course, the process of improving settings need not be as elaborate as in this case. It may be as simple as allowing people to arrange furniture in an employee lounge in the way they wish, or replacing lighting fixtures that have made an area so unpleasant that people stay away from it whenever possible.

2. *Changing Physical Settings to Support a Social System Organization Development Process.* My interest in sociophysical approaches to change grew out of this particular application. In the course of organization development activities with different organizations, I became more and more aware of the impact physical facilities were having on whether our plans for social changes were actually being carried out. For instance, one factory had attempted to encourage group decision-making at the machine-operators' level and below, yet there was no space available where a group larger than six people could get together. It was clear that we needed to create such a space if we expected meetings to be held. Another example has been provided by my work with universities. The structure of most classrooms and lecture halls tends to coerce a particular kind of social system in a class: teacher-dominated, little connection among peers, and passivity in the learning process. The school that tries to change this climate without giving attention to its physical structure will be fighting against both human resistance and the signals of the physical surroundings.

Lately, I have been concerned with a similar problem on a larger scale: the trend in the United States toward changing the orientation of the prison system from one of punishment to one of rehabilitation.

Although I have done no first-hand work with this change process, I have thought about its problems from the standpoint of the six functions:

> In general, most prisons have been designed with very clear spatial-decision rules: they should be negative on *pleasure* and *growth*, since this is what an enemy of society deserves; they should be rich in *symbolic* messages which say that the inmate is reprehensible and that he is powerless when compared with the (supposedly) conscientious will of the society as a whole; they should *shelter* society from the prisoner, and it is immaterial if the prisoner is not sheltered from physical and psychological stresses; they should make it difficult to carry out any *tasks* in the prison, thus reinforcing the message that the prisoner is unproductive; and they should continually threaten *social contact* needs through the practice of putting the prisoner in "solitary confinement."
>
> It should be clear from this brief description that any attempt to shift the institution of penology from a custodial and punishment function toward a rehabilitative function will be difficult if the physical structures are not changed in the process. In their present form, these structures strongly reinforce a degradation of the prisoner's self-image, whereas the goal of rehabilitation would be to enhance that self-image to the point where the prisoner no longer feels the need to engage in antisocial behavior.
>
> A nice case of what I am suggesting comes from a recent newspaper article (Anon., 1971): "If an inmate of Britain's newest prison wants to tack pinups to the wall of his centrally heated cell he will find a bulletin board there for the purpose. Should he crave privacy, he need only lock his cell door with his own key, although the cell will be double-locked by the guard." The designers of this prison stated later that they were trying to reduce the custodial aspect and loosen up the system for more therapeutic work.
>
> I believe that they are on the right track by changing the *symbolic* messages of the setting. They have also increased *shelter* and *security* for the prisoners, through both central heating and the ability to lock others *out* of their cell. The bulletin board works on both the *pleasure* and the *symbolic* functions, since the men can now decorate their cells.
>
> This example is in direct contrast with the experience of a colleague with a state prison board in the United States. The board professed to

> be interested in rehabilitation, yet it took him over a year to get them to try the experiment of allowing a small group of prisoners to rearrange the bed, table, and chair in their cells. As long as they say they are interested in a new prison climate, yet are unwilling to alter the rules and surroundings that support that climate, including the way spatial decisions are made, it is unlikely that very much will change in the world of the prisoner.

The danger in this last case is one that exists for every organization development project, namely the "half-trial." By this I mean the process whereby an organization's power figures reluctantly decide to try to develop the human resources potential of their system, then balk at instituting the concurrent changes needed to support this development. Then, when not much change occurs, the project is termed unsound. It should, instead, suggest that the project was never really tried. I believe that attention to the physical dimension is an important element in avoiding the half-trial organization development project.

3. *Using Sociophysical Approaches to Enhance the Problem-Solving Ability of a Client System.* Throughout this book I have urged the case for spatial problem-solving as a good training ground for more general skills, because of its concreteness and visibility. My experience has been that teaching clients the six-functions system for diagnosis has also encouraged them to take a costs-gains approach in other problem areas, as well as helped them make better spatial decisions. This outcome is discussed in detail in the following three chapters, which deal with enhancing environmental competence.

4. *Using Organization Development Processes to Facilitate Physical-Setting Changes.* This is in a sense the mirror image of the other applications that I have mentioned. It simply means that the knowledge we are now developing about social system change processes could be put to good use in helping physical alterations to succeed. Every system must replace its facilities as they wear out or become inadequate, and attention to the change process itself will help the system ensure that the change will be one for the better. For instance, in Manning's (1965) study of a new office building, he found that new facilities had an interesting effect on the climate:

> The discussion of the new building often led to considerable talk about staff/management relations. Many people felt that these had

> suffered with the move into the new building. There was a feeling that the rank and file were being regimented. "It's more like the army now," and, "There are too many regulations; it was very easygoing before."
>
> This appeared to be due, in part, to the management's and supervisors' zeal to keep everything crisp and tidy; to ban any personal effects; and to insist on desks being tidied every night. The new, more autocratic form of supervision was regarded as being a consequence of the large offices, which, it was felt, foster a passion for symmetrical layouts and obsessional tidiness.[1]

Put simply, a change to better quarters does not necessarily lead to a better managerial or social climate; it may do just the opposite. In the case above, a consultant would have been quite helpful in confronting the issue of the trade-off between conserving the new facilities and deteriorating the social climate that they were designed to improve. Similarly, the use of other organization development techniques such as intergroup sessions, norm diagnosis, and quick opinion-gathering and sharing will increase the likelihood that the possibilities of a new physical setting will be realized.

SOME FINAL REMINDERS

In closing this chapter on applications of the sociophysical approach, there are several general points that I would like to restate. One is that the rating system is not geared to tell you automatically whether a setting is good or bad. It is designed to clarify what the consequences of a setting are. These consequences can then be compared with what you want in order to decide what needs to be changed.

Second, the goal of a spatial diagnostic process is, as I conceive it, to put yourself into the world of the user as much as possible – not to simply impose, in the guise of good taste, your own tastes and fantasies upon the user.

Finally, as I said earlier, there is no substitute in this area for getting out into the client system and moving around in the system's spaces. Work on the sociophysical approach to change cannot be done in an armchair or in a remote, hotel conference room; as Professor Harold Hill put it in *The Music Man*, "You have got to know the territory."

---

1 Manning, *op. cit.*, p. 479. Reprinted by permission.

Part 3
TOWARD ENVIRONMENTAL COMPETENCE

11
ENVIRONMENTAL COMPETENCE: CONCEPTS

In this final section of the book I will focus on a specific target for change – the ability of individuals and organizations to use the full potential of their physical settings. From my own observations, I realize that most people both underutilize the potential of their settings and tend to accept inappropriate settings. In the next two chapters I will focus on blocks to the environmental competence of individuals and small groups, and on methods for enhancing environmental competence. In the final chapter I will discuss organizations' processes of making decisions about settings – organizational environmental competence.

ENVIRONMENTAL COMPETENCE

Earlier in this book I defined environmental competence as: (a) a person's ability to be aware of the surrounding environment and its impact on him; and (b) his ability to use or change his settings to help him achieve his goals without inappropriately destroying the setting or reducing his sense of effectiveness or that of the people around him.[1]

---

1 I say "inappropriately destroying the setting" because using up some places and things is more fitting than saving them for eternity at the expense of vitality of present use.

The consultant's goals in enhancing environmental competence thus are twofold: first, to improve the client's utilization of resources; and second, to increase the client's competence in the world and his ability to solve different kinds of problems, in addition to those about physical settings. Earlier, I illustrated how environmental features are a good medium for improving one's problem-solving skills: physical settings are visible, changes are usually immediately discernable, and it is possible to get rapid feedback about the effect of those changes. These features are important because the process of [sensing a problem ⟶ problem-solving ⟶ action ⟶ feedback about consequences] leads to growth, i.e., increased competence.

AWARENESS OF POSSIBILITIES

For many people in organizations, this chain never begins. Since they are unaware that a problem exists, they are also oblivious to alternatives that could improve, for example, the present condition of the walls, the current assignment of offices, or the present lighting arrangement.

In *The Hidden Dimension*, Hall summarizes features of the environment and assigns them to two categories:

–*Fixed-Feature Space*, that is, physical features that are relatively nonchangeable and nonmoveable. Examples are load-bearing walls, monuments, boulders, streets, and floors.

–*Semi-Fixed-Feature Space*, i.e., elements that are changeable in either form or location, such as chairs, pictures, desks, rugs, and drapes.

Both of these categories are derived from inherent properties of the elements. In addition, we can look at an element's fixedness in subjective or psychological terms. In so doing, a third category emerges, one which to me is the most interesting for examining environmental competence:

–*Pseudo-Fixed-Feature Space* $(PFF)^2$, i.e., those features in man's environment that are relatively simple to change or move, but which are perceived as fixed, even when their configuration is inappropriate for task accomplishment. In most group and organizational settings, there are a great many changeable features (technically speaking) which are treated as if they were fixed.

PSEUDO-FIXED FEATURES

There are many examples of PFF space which could be cited, but let us consider just a few here. We have all noted that people entering a room for a meeting rarely rearrange the furniture. Similarly, newly formed T-groups (self-analytic learning groups) do not alter the physical setting until the group members begin to be self-conscious about their behavior and choice-points. Once they realize that they have taken the setting as given, they begin to experiment with changes in the setting. Then there is a great deal of excitement about trying new seating arrangements, using tables in new ways or removing them, and other tangible kinds of experimentation and exploration.

As another example, the board rooms of many organizations often contain tables which can be made larger or smaller, depending on the size of the group. I have never seen a group that has been meeting in one of these rooms ever change the size of the table, even when such a change would have been quite appropriate. There were once five of us around a 20-foot table with four sections in it; making the table smaller would have made a great deal more sense and would have facilitated our establishing a less stiff and formal relationship.

Another obvious example of a possible alteration in the environment is the placement of lighting in a room. How many of us have left a lamp in a particular position, although we might have preferred to read or write in a different part of the room?

A final example is quite striking in its implications for the design process and for the flexible use of space. In the new Ford Foundation Building a norm developed that the curtains, which were designed to screen the offices' glass walls when the users wanted privacy, should be left undrawn to indicate that the person had nothing to hide. That is, a design

---

2 Although the features of a space may be "pseudo-fixed" to the users, these same features may be regarded as "pseudo-variable" to the designer or creator of that space (who see it as changeable, although the inhabitors do not use it that way). I have developed the notions here from the point of view of the user, since he is the "problem-solver" with whom I am concerned; hence, the use of PFF. It is obvious that these are not completely separate categories. An architect recently said to me: "I'm designing a unit that can be altered or shifted for different moods or needs – it is a richer environment." My view is different; an environment will not *be* "richer" until people *use* the variations and bring the potential richness out of it.

feature which was created to give people a *choice* about how they would like to use their own space – open and public or closed and private – actually inhibited choice because of social norms. The glass walls and the open drapes became what I am calling PFF – pseudo-fixed-features.

My reason for going into such detail is that a great leverage for change exists if we understand more about the PFF phenomenon. A change in attitudes or behavior about space problems, especially variable features of space, will lead to a much greater utilization of resources, better fit between activities and the spatial environment, and a richer existential learning process. This process, if it continues, will also make flexible design processes more exciting, and more creative energy will be put into environmental design, since designers will *believe* that people can and will use the design features of settings in creative ways.

PROBLEM-SOLVING AND THE ENVIRONMENT

What are the alternatives to the PFF mode of functioning? One possibility is a problem-solving approach which requires the user to ask such questions as: "Is the physical setting right for what we want to do now?" "What could be changed to improve the setting?" "Can these changes be made easily with what we have or with what we can get with relatively little effort?" In other words, spatial problem-solving involves several steps: (a) asking what we are trying to *do* in the setting; (b) asking what spatial arrangements would be adequate or useful for our purposes; (c) specifying the present spatial arrangement and comparing it with our needs; (d) asking what can be done to change the setting to make it more appropriate and how much energy is required to carry out the changes; (e) choosing an alternative and acting on it; and (f) making note of the consequences of our choices for inclusion in future problem-solving tasks.

Unfortunately, groups and organizations rarely ask these questions. When they are raised, these questions often get put aside before they can be handled directly. The steps listed above encourage greater exploration of a group's work settings and their influence on moods and interaction patterns. An additional outcome of this process is the potential for people to learn more about themselves and the world. Spatial problem-solving promotes individual growth; one learns how to consider alternatives, how to look at things, what he wants in physical spaces, and what the outcomes were from his activities. Just asking "What do I want to do here?" is often a growth-producing mechanism. Finally, as both our population and the percentage of people living in metropolitan areas increase, it becomes increasingly important to influence our immediate environmental surroundings. Unless we have greater inclination to do this, our cities and suburbs may soon become psychologically uninhabitable for all except those able to afford great luxuries in space and materials.

CAUSES OF PFF ASSUMPTIONS

Why does problem-solving about space occur so rarely? Why do people define space in PFF terms? We obviously need a great deal of research in order to provide good, solid answers to these questions. However, it is possible at this time to make some general statements. The preponderance of PFF space arises from two main sources: characteristics of the individual and characteristics of the social setting or climate.

Individual Characteristics

1. Some people have nonproblem-solving personalities; they are nonproactive – passively influenced by the world. For example, Rotter's (1966) research indicates that there are generalized personal tendencies to perceive reinforcement or effects as either linked to one's own behavior or controlled by external forces. A person with the latter tendency is less likely to actively influence his surroundings than is one who sees the relationship between his experiences and his actions. The nonproactive person needs some psychologically successful experiences that enhance his sense of personal effectiveness to reduce his PFF behavior.

2. In addition to resignation at being unable to influence what goes on around them, people may hold PFF assumptions *because they are unaware of their experiences or feelings*. One example of this is the childhood amnesia described by Schachtel (1959). As I noted in Chapter 8, people in our culture are encouraged to develop stereotyped schemata for dealing with their experiences. These schemata do not focus on present feelings, but rather on how events will be described in the future. Thus, with the passage of time the person is less likely to recognize and deal with the deficiencies in his physical settings. He lacks motivation to think about how an altered setting might produce better experiences for him; in fact, "better experiences" would be meaningless to him.

Several people, such as Perls *et al.* (1951) and Schutz (1968) have developed experience-based training methods designed specifically to reconnect people with the experiences of both their internal and external worlds. Similarly, I have developed a set of exercises to expand a person's awareness of his experiences in an office setting. These exercises will be presented in the next chapter.

3. Even when we are aware of our experiences, we tend to have difficulty relating them to spatial causes; we are *blind to the impact of settings*. It is with good reason that Hall refers to a "*hidden* dimension" in his excellent book on spatial effects. We lack the ability to look at our physical surroundings and their influences on us, and the necessary training is provided by neither our educational institutions nor work organizations. However, the recent exploration of consciousness-expanding experiences (through drugs, "happenings", light shows, and other media) is the start of a strong trend away from blindness to the effects of the environment.

4. A fourth factor affecting a person's inability to solve spatial problems is his *lack of concrete knowledge* about the technology of changing the variable features of a space. If someone does not know how to change something, he is unlikely to consider changing it. Tables, partitions, chairs, etc., that might be placed in various locations rarely get moved, due to the user's lack of knowledge about the possibilities. If the person *feels* unknowledgeable, he usually divorces himself from the change process and leaves it to the "experts," who are often even less knowledgeable about his needs. How-to-do-it magazines are popular in part because they dissipate one's feelings of inferiority and inability.

5. People often are *not clear about what they want or what they are trying to do*, thus making it difficult for them to define an "appropriate" setting. Similarly, people may have some notion of what a space should be like, yet be unable to *articulate* their ideas; the languages of both personal goals and space are much too scanty at present. Also, the "form follows function" rule does not help much if one cannot define the function. Asking a client to specify what he wants on the six spatial functions often helps him clarify his wishes about both his setting and his goals.

6. Sometimes an individual seems to be *motivated to maintain his inadequate environment*. My hypothesis is that a person does this because he feels (usually unconsciously) that it is more congruent with his low

self-worth; that is, a person who believes himself to be of little value feels that he *deserves* to be in "crummy" surroundings. He may, in fact, then rule out actions which would improve his surroundings, thereby reinforcing and acting out his self-concept.

This is a particularly strong component in the way slum areas begin to deteriorate after renewal; the residents believe that they deserve to live in a deteriorating place of little value. Thus, one of the first steps toward social change should be to help the residents improve their sense of self-worth rather than to change the physical surroundings. The physical environment could be used as a tool to enhance the residents' self-worth – their influencing something in the environment could help create a sense of competence. In this light the renewal process is too important to be given to anyone but those who need it most – the residents. In the chapter on decision-making, I will discuss the importance of this point of view for office design and change.

7. Another motivational factor has to do with a person's sense of the usefulness of influencing his setting. In many instances *the impact of the physical environment is considered a marginal concern*. The user judges that too much energy is needed to think about how to change the setting, given the importance of his current task. In many instances this is quite true; there are more important things at hand. However, this condition can be managed. When someone asks "Is the setting right?", it takes just a few seconds to say that it is adequate for what we are doing at the moment.

The problem is that in practice, the notion of "it's not worth the energy" gets carried back one step. That particular assumption blocks even *asking* whether the setting is appropriate. People assume in advance that they already know the answer. In some instances this assumption is just not true; a change in the physical space will have an important impact on the quantity and quality of what is being produced, on the kinds of experiences people are having, etc. To assume that the setting's impact is marginal dismisses the problem and makes it difficult to envision what a place would have been like had it been changed.

Goffman (1963) discusses an interesting related phenomenon, i.e., group norms may prohibit a person's expressing concern about spatial factors, on the assumption that his role in the proceedings calls for him to *look* fully involved in the main task. It often is immaterial whether the space is hindering the main task; the person is still expected to express his interest in the main task rather than in the surroundings.

8. Finally, there is what I call, for lack of a more elegant phrase, the *fear of messing something up*. We often feel that a change in the physical setting, such as painting a wall, is irreversible. Consequently, we want something to be perfect the first time and then left as is. We are unfamiliar with the notion of settings as ever-changing, evolving, and experimental. This lack of understanding makes us wary of actually starting to change something, because we might somehow reduce its value or have to make replacements.

This cautiousness may also be a result of the "Protestant Ethic" concept of saving which, in the extreme, means preserving something that could be functional now for someone who never uses it because it is always being saved. In some church institutions the use of the physical facilities is discouraged, apparently because they are being preserved for eternity. Researchers could probably discover ties between an individual's fear of failure in making spatial changes and his early family experiences and fantasies about parental expectations of perfection.

Social Factors

A second set of PFF factors, attributes of the *social* setting, is present in addition to the physical environment.

1. One clear factor is the *set of norms about acceptable behavior* in a group or organization. Group norms often inhibit initiation, changes, or concrete suggestions for doing something as a group. If a person who makes a suggestion is mocked or put down, he will be unlikely to raise the issue of an inappropriate physical setting for fear that he may be laughed at or accused of having an ulterior motive.

Similarly, norms about the degree of confrontation and discussion of group-process issues will affect spatial problem-solving and influence the tendency to adopt PFF assumptions. The following is a potent example of this kind of inhibition:

> A member of a president's staff group told me that the group's use of space created a rigid, formal atmosphere in which only certain people could be active and grow. The staff members always sat in the same seats, and reports were always given starting with the person on the president's left. This meant that the same people always spoke first, second, etc., and others almost never spoke, because all the topics had been exhausted. Yet he also told me that he would never raise the seating issue in the group; that would be a bigger *faux pas* than

inappropriate seating, since it would raise the taboo subject of power relations in the group.

The only thing worse than deviating from a spatial norm was to speak openly about the norm in the group. As in many systems, the president was the only member who could change the seating pattern without being chastised by the group.

2. A second social factor is *disagreement over goals*. This often occurs when something in the physical setting remains unchanged because the status quo is less uncertain than change. If there is a lack of agreement about what is trying to be done in a group setting, there is probably even less agreement about an appropriate physical setting. Therefore, inertia turns out to be the biggest factor in maintaining the status quo.

3. The third social factor in PFF assumptions is the concept of *territoriality* (see Altman and Haythorn, 1967; Ardrey, 1966). We rarely think of changing something in the environment if it is on someone else's "turf," e.g., correcting inappropriate lighting, moving furniture, and the like. I think this is generally true for people at home, in the office setting, and in public spaces. If we have a sense of outsidership and nonownership, we feel that we ought to keep quiet and that we have no right to try to influence the impact someone else's setting is having on us. For example, in the case I cited earlier of the consulting team that was not able to hold a unified group meeting in a client's living room, group formation was not blocked by the arrangement of seats *per se*, but rather by the consultants' feeling that it would be inappropriate to suggest rearranging the furniture.

A costly kind of PFF territoriality is exhibited in the hierarchical structure of many organizations. If an organization's culture defines certain areas as "off limits" to lower- or upper-level members, that area is a refuge for those who *can* use it, but the activities that can take place in that setting are limited. For instance, in one client organization, there was a very fine meeting room which could be used only by the executive committee for its twice-monthly, two-hour meetings. The symbolic gain of a special territory for the committee carried a high price in a system where there were few good meeting spaces.

4. The final social factor is in a sense the opposite of those already mentioned, all of which imply that a group exists with norms and some form of organization. People make PFF assumptions *when they are part of a collectivity rather than a group.* For instance, people in a doctor's waiting

room are a collectivity; their presence in the same room does not define a social system. Travelers in an airport lounge are also a collectivity. By contrast, a work team has a developed culture with norms, processes for decision-making, and the like.

In collectivities, people tend to make very few changes in the setting. My hypothesis is that people in collectivities have even less information than they do in groups about how others will feel about them if they make a change in the setting. The collectivity has no established conflict-resolution mechanisms (first-come, seniority, position, etc.) if contradictory wishes become visible. All of these factors mean that the low-risk alternative is to simply take things as they are, so that everyone "makes do" with a setting which remains unchanged from its initial design.

12

ENHANCING ENVIRONMENTAL COMPETENCE: SOME SUGGESTED METHODS

Having discussed the main reasons why people do not use the full potential of their settings, I will now turn to some methodologies for enhancing individuals' environmental competence. These methods were chosen for their usefulness in increasing people's ability to both *use* the potential of settings and *choose* settings appropriate to their needs. Of course, there are many ways that spatial training might occur. The ones that I have found most useful are: didactic teaching of the six-functions model, experiential exercises with a person or group in the organization's spaces, involving clients with designers, seeking out and increasing the experimentation of the "influentials" in a group, and the use of spatial factors in on-going process consultation.

TEACHING THE SIX FUNCTIONS

One of the most direct ways to increase a person's awareness of an area that influences him, such as space, is to provide him with categories for sorting out phenomena. This usually improves his ability to make choices about what he wants in that area, as well as increases his awareness of the setting. This view is supported by McClelland's (1961) studies, in which he found that one of the most direct ways to increase a person's achievement motivation was to teach him the coding system for scoring achievement motivation on the Thematic Apperception Test. An understanding of the operational definition of the concept of achievement motivation tended to change his subjects' perception of the world and their relation to it.

Similarly, I have found that one of the most direct ways to help a client become more aware of his relation to his physical settings is to teach him the six-functions model described in Chapters 4 through 9. Although it is not a tightly connected theoretical structure, the six-functions model does provide a set of categories by which he can sort out what had been a relatively jumbled, nonpatterned set of experiences.

I usually begin with a small group, to avoid having to repeat the same thing to each individual. I present descriptions of each function; then, I ask the group members to move around and practice rating different elements on the various dimensions. This usually occurs in an organization's spaces, since I try to do this kind of training in the places where the clients work. (However, I have also had people practice outdoors, in public buildings, and in homes.) It has been helpful to have people try to be particularly aware of different dimensions, assessing what people lose when one element rates high on one dimension, e.g., an elegant reception area in which visitors maintain silence and therefore do not interact. After 30 minutes to an hour, the group reassembles to share observations, look at conflicting ratings, and attempt to clarify definitions.

This process, plus practice and repeated sharing of ratings has, in my experience, helped clients become much more aware of the shape and influence of their settings. The six-functions model helps a person take a more subtle view of this influence process, helping him to realize that a physical element can be useful to him on one dimension and a hindrance on another, or that an element is positive for him on pleasure and negative for someone else, and so on. This complex view helps him to make conscious choices about what he wants to get from his settings and is therefore willing to give up in order to get it.

EXPERIENTIAL TRAINING EXERCISES

A related method for increasing environmental competence is to structure laboratory-style exercises so that people can use spatial experiences to learn about themselves, their settings, and their social system. If a consultant has built the appropriate relationship with a client group, he could use the exercises that follow to create a "micro-laboratory" (short-term training program) on the impact of physical settings.

The following exercises are a combination of actions to perform (in italics) and questions that heighten attention to specific spatial experiences. The questions are also useful for sharing experiences in a group and comparing similarities and differences in individual responses. To demonstrate how the exercises work in practice, I have interspersed (in parentheses) some responses that I have been given while using these exercises. I should also add that these exercises are not meant to be rigidly applied as a whole, on either a client system or yourself. The exercises are not intended to be complete as they stand, but should be adapted to the particular situation – size of group, time constraints, experience of the people, and so on. (Many exercises could be designed to get at issues other than those illustrated here.)[1]

General Sensitivity to the Setting

Just walk around your whole setting for ten to fifteen minutes, trying to see as much as possible without staring so hard that you don't allow new images to come to mind. Try to be open to seeing new patterns or relationships of things, places, and people. *It would be helpful to do this at least twice – once during the most active part of the day in your work area, and again when it is deserted.* Compare the differences in the setting at those two times. *Also, get two or three others to do this with you, then share what you have seen and how you felt about it.* Do you like the things you see? Which ones? Which areas do you dislike? Why? Where are there major differences – is there an area that evokes very different feelings from different people? Can you talk about it enough to discover why the reactions are so different to those places? ("I noticed that there are several areas that I never go to unless I can't help it. I realize now that it's because they feel bad or depressing to me. I wonder how the people who work in there all the time feel about it.")

Social Contact

Move around your work setting again, but this time try to be particularly aware of the impact of spaces or layouts on the ways people interact (or do not). Given this layout, who is it easy or difficult to talk with on short notice? Who would you like to be able to talk with more easily than you can now? What kinds of changes in layout would be necessary to make

---

1 See "Contacting the Environment," pp. 30-72 in Perls, Hefferline, and Goodman, *Gestalt Therapy*. New York: Julian Press, 1951.

that possible? Is it things, locations of people, your own feelings, or the other person's feelings that need to be changed in order for this to happen?

Look for unclaimed areas where people can get together to chat informally for a few minutes without being in anyone's space. Do people tend to do this here? What kinds of places do they use – open spaces, corridors, lounges, outdoor areas, or meeting rooms? Would it help to have some other alternatives and if so, where would these spaces be? ("We don't have any free space except the reception area, and we're not supposed to talk there because visitors would overhear us.")

Where can groups of various sizes get together? What is the largest size group that could be handled by the spaces that now exist in the setting? What is the largest grouping that does in fact get together? Are the large spaces actually available, or are there understood rules about what can and cannot happen in them? ("We can use the cafeteria for large meetings." "That's only for Employee Association or other similar things, though. I've never seen it used for a work meeting." "I guess we could use the hallway! Every other place is too cut up into cubicles or filled up with machinery.")

Symbolic Identification, Personal Places

Do you have a "place" in your work setting? *The next time you are in it, take a good look at it.* What are its boundaries – where does your place end and someone else's begin? What features identify it as your place? Are others who know you well able to tell that it is yours by looking at it, or do they know this only because they see you in it regularly? Would someone who did not know you well be able to tell that this place was different from the ones near it? ("Not really. Even my one poster looks like the others outside my office. I haven't made much visible difference.") *Identify some people at work who use their desks or offices to create a setting that is very clearly their own place.* What kinds of things have they done? *If no one comes to mind, walk around a bit and see if you can now see such a place.* What specifically have they done to create that sense of identity between themselves and their place? (I like the place where Suzie[2] hung that rug on the wall beside her desk. It feels warm and cozy.")

---

2 Fictitious names have been used throughout the comments.

If you have done relatively little to personalize your own place, *think for a few minutes about the reasons.* ("I never thought of it." "I haven't got any talent for that sort of thing." "I'll be leaving here soon so it isn't worth the trouble" [said one person who had been in his present office for eighteen months]. "There are rules against doing anything to the stuff here, because someone else will have to use it after me.") *When you have made your list, evaluate the reasons as you now see them.* Do other alternatives for what you might do now come to mind? Can you do something fairly simple to your place that will make it seem more like yours?

Move around the setting again and try to be aware of who has been most able to express himself in his space. Who has done this the least? Why were some able to do this? Was it creativity, luck, power, or what? Who are the people in this organization or group who seem to set the patterns in the use of spaces, facilities, and furniture? Are there obvious trend-setters, or is that unclear? ("I have trouble seeing anybody as very free in their use of their place. Even the vice-president has mostly company-approved furnishings, and they're arranged just the way they were when Hopkins was there before him." "Only Jim has anything personal. He brought his own chair to use at his machine.")

Symbolic Identification to Outsiders

Try entering your building, plant, or workyard as a visitor might, and try to feel as he might. Also do this with a friend who has never been there, and get his reactions to it. When someone new comes in, what messages does he get about where he should go, what people work there, what activities take place there, what the climate of the organization is like, and so on? ("I did this with my wife, who had never actually been inside my building. She said that it had a much colder feeling than the picture she got from reading the company newspaper, but pretty close to the feeling she got from my comments.")

Tasks, PFF Assumptions, and Growth

Think now about how people use the facilities – spaces, desks, rooms, machines, walkways, decorations, and so on. What kinds of norms and formal rules exist about how things can be used or changed here? Are there particular things that cannot be done, such as painting, bringing in your own furnishings, moving things around, or holding certain kinds of meetings in spaces that are designated "for" something else? Where do these rules come from? ("I guess it's an unwritten law that only vice-presidents can use Room 1256 – nobody else has ever tried to use it." "We can't repaint because the owner of the building has it in the company's contract that alterations won't be made without his approval." "Well, it looks like a lot of the constraints are our own, things we assume can't be done. There are some common customs about what you do with your desk, chairs, and whatever.")

Think also about how decisions about space, locations, decorations, arrangements, and the like get made in your setting. Which decisions are yours, which are the group's, and which ones are influenced by someone who is not present? *Talk with some others, including your boss, about how the setting got the way it is, and see whether people know how decisions were made about various facilities.* In many organizations these decisions are made anonymously, and everyone assumes that someone must have had a "good reason." Are there some things in the setting about which you wish you had more control or influence? What are they, and who can affect them now? Do you really have as little possibility for influence as you have thought? ("This has made me think of some changes I might make that don't really require anybody's approval – like I'm going to turn my desk around." "I still don't see what I could have different. I can't hang anything up, because I have no wall, and we're not allowed to clutter up the aisles near our benches – so what could I do?")

In thinking about what kinds of changes you could make, *try also to be aware of those decisions which will affect other people*, such as hanging posters on the outside of your office or wanting to paint a common wall green. Who are the people most directly affected, and can you get together with them and reach some agreement about what you want to do?

Messages About Desired Interaction

Ask several people who come into your space regularly to describe the messages they get from your setting about how you expect them to act with you and what the mood of the relationship should be. Most people use their desks, chairs, and other objects as props to establish a mood or climate for relationships with other people – moods of closeness or distance, business concern or pleasure, and many others. Study the messages your props communicate. ("Two people told me that the way I fiddle with my tools always tells them to get out as soon as possible.")

Symbolic Identification About Status

Take another walk around your work spaces, preferably with one or two other people, and try to find all the status symbols that tell you where people stand in the organization. Every organization develops its own language about the facilities that imply importance or status. *Make a list of the status factors* (size of office, having an office, size of desk, location, and so on), *and have your friends do the same.* Is there general agreement about the signals of status for different levels? If not, what causes the confusion – do different areas have different rules, or are there no such clear differentiations in the system to begin with? ("Frankly, mostly older employees are confused now, because I and several other newer people don't go along with the old language. I brought in a throw rug for my office, which throws some people way off.")

Try also to look at the symbolic language and see what has to be given up in functionality in order to maintain the language and relative positions. For instance, does a man have to get a bigger desk when he is promoted to a certain level, even if he can then no longer hold meetings in his office? How flexible or rigid is the system about someone's rejecting new "rewards" that would get in the way of his doing his job? And, on the other hand, is the system flexible enough to allow someone to use his own props (such as the throw rug), thus making the space more comfortable for himself and others, but at the same time implying (if the props were furnished by the company) that he is higher in the hierarchy than he actually is?

Interaction and Shelter

Pick a busy time of day in your organization and ask a friend in your work group to help you. Try to hold a truly private conversation in four or five different places in your work setting. Your office or desk area should be one, but try to find several others. How easy or difficult is it to find other places? How good is your own space for intimate, private conversations? Have there been many times when you did not say what you wanted to because there was no good place in which to say it? Do you think others feel the same way? *Ask some other people how they feel about the privacy that is possible in the office and where they go when they want privacy.* ("This was hard to do. There was only one place we could really feel comfortable, and that was in his office. Mine has walls that are so thin I hear every telephone conversation on either side, so they must hear mine." "We go to a coffee shop when we want real privacy.")

In addition to private conversations, another obvious form of privacy is the opportunity to get off by yourself in order to think, concentrate, daydream, or relax. Are there places in your setting where you can do that? Does your space serve that function, and is it possible to buffer yourself against interruptions? For example, some groups have developed signal flags similar to those on ships to indicate when they do not want to be interrupted. If this is not possible where you work, what do you think are the effects on you? Can you remember instances of wanting very much to have that privacy and yet feeling unable to achieve it? How did you resolve this problem, or did it just remain as a frustration that had to be compensated for in some other way, e.g., getting out of town for the weekend? Are there some alternatives which could be built into the space that would allow more of this privacy when you wanted it? ("I get to a point and then I've had it – I just go out for a walk. I don't care what my supervisor thinks, you can't be looked at all day every day!")

In closing this section, I want to repeat that these activities and questions should be tailored to the particular situation in which they are to be used. I also hope that readers will create awareness-expanding activities of their own.

COLLABORATION WITH DESIGNERS

As a group, designers tend to be more aware of settings and spaces than is the average person. They therefore represent a resource for the consultant. Design-trained people should be used as part of a change team in the organization development process. They could be of great help in decision-making about physical structures, but they could be even more important in helping the client system expand its perceptions of the possibilities inherent in a particular design. This is a departure from the traditional definition of the architect's or designer's role, which ends with the completion of the "thing" and a "good luck" wish that it be used well. To involve designers in the user's process seems to me to be only a simple application of the consulting principle of bringing client needs and resources together.

INFLUENCING THE INFLUENTIALS

An interesting process of social change that has been empirically observed in communities is the "two-step flow of communication" described by Katz and Lazarsfeld (1955). In this process key people in a community set a trend which then provides a kind of "all clear" signal for others, who then also adopt the change in attitude or behavior. I have observed a similar phenomenon in organizations, where people take their cues as to what is permissible or look for new alternatives from the "influentials."

This suggests that if a consultant wants to expand a group's ability to use its facilities in flexible or creative ways, he can use the influentials in that group as a medium for change. If he can identify (through observing or asking) the style leaders in that group, he can work with them to start expanding the effectiveness of spatial behavior in the whole group.

PROCESS CONSULTATION

In helping people become more skilled at influencing their surroundings, it is not necessary to be always working directly on environmental competence. Perhaps the greatest number of opportunities to enhance clients' competent use of facilities comes when a consultant is engaged in what Schein (1969) has labelled "process consultation," i.e., the consultant is present for the on-going activities of a work group rather than for special change-oriented events.

My suggestion is that the spatial dimension be included in both process observations, which the consultant shares with clients, and consultant interventions aimed at changes in process. For instance, I once remarked to a group that we had not moved the chairs closer together when we entered the room, even though such a change would have been appropriate for the size of the group. This observation created a feeling of closeness within the group and served as a reminder to ask how the room should be arranged before starting future meetings.

Attention to spatial factors is important and can be used during almost any consultation with a client. Although this point may seem somewhat obvious, I have mentioned it here because my observation is that consultants, as well as clients, tend to omit the impact of the setting when trying to increase individual and group effectiveness.

WHERE TO START

In closing this chapter I want to mention one step that has been only implied: a consultant should start with *himself* – increasing his awareness of spatial dimensions, discovering blocks to problem-solving, and exploring new alternatives. Only if he is able to be experimental in this medium is he likely to be able to increase these qualities in his clients.

13 ORGANIZATIONAL ENVIRONMENTAL COMPETENCE: SPATIAL DECISION PROCESSES

In this final chapter I will describe another factor which contributes to a system's effectiveness in structuring and using its physical facilities – the processes by which spatial decisions are made in the organization. If a consultant has a clear view of how facilities decisions are being made in a system, he can work directly on these decision processes. In the long run this will have more impact on the health of the system and its members than will any specific structural decisions which the consultant influences. My goal here is to increase the system's ability to solve problems rather than to solve specific problems for the system.

SPATIAL-DECISION PROCESSES IN ORGANIZATIONS TODAY

The dominant pattern in making decisions about physical facilities is clearly one of top-down, high-control decision-making. This is true for both large- and small-scale decisions. Large-scale decisions about location, general layout, type of office decor, and locations of people are nearly always made by the top management level. For smaller-scale decisions, many organizations either require that members get prior clearance or prohibit any changes in individual offices or spaces. For example,

> A middle-level manager decided that his desk had faced the door of his office for too long. It was time for a change, so he turned it around to face a side wall. The next day he found a memo on his desk from the president's assistant saying that it had been found that the most effective way for managers to arrange their offices was with the desk facing the door so others would feel welcome. He was instructed to return his desk to its old position, with the firmly implied threat of no longer being considered an effective manager if he did not. He later discovered that there was only one exception to the desk-toward-the-door rule: the president's office!

At one level the message this manager received was that he had encroached on the symbolic territory of the president, namely, the desk arrangement. More important, however, he also received a higher-level message, which he described as follows:

> What I noticed most was not that our desks had to be different, but that our freedom to arrange our desks was so different. Can you imagine him (the president) getting a memo because he moved *his* stuff around??!!

This message of lack of control over one's own work surroundings is often institutionalized by company policy, as in the following example:

> One major national company had a famous design firm create a new building for them, including an "integrated" interior design for all executive offices. A written rule stipulated that *no* changes could be made in any of the executive offices without the approval of the president.

This company is not so different from many other organizations today, except possibly in the openness with which it maintains control. It is still assumed that the "system" (those higher in the hierarchy) must take responsibility for the facilities of individual members and groups, presumably because they cannot take responsibility for themselves. In many organizations it is still true that the president and his staff and the cleaning crew (for reasons I will discuss later) exert the most influence over physical settings. Lower-level employees and middle-management levels tend to have relatively less influence over their own settings than do either of these other groups.

BLOCKS TO A GREATER RANGE OF SPATIAL DECISION STYLES

If we assume that the description above is reasonably accurate, the most important diagnostic issue in attempting to weaken the norm of unilateral, top-down decisions about settings is the reason for so little power-sharing in this area. There are a number of important factors that contribute to this pattern.

Executive Values About Individual-Organization Relations

Many powerful members of systems still hold what McGregor (1960) called "Theory X" assumptions about human nature, i.e., people shy away from work, avoid responsibility, and must be controlled in order to get them to behave in ways that will meet the organization's needs. Physical facilities are often the most visible arena for observing these Theory X assumptions, particularly in companies where top management has been "turned on" to more humanistic values about self-control but has not internalized these values. They talk about their new approach, yet continue to make spatial decisions unilaterally, as if these decisions did not count in the new game.

Fears About Conflict

Many executives assume that their subordinates' level of interpersonal competence is low. They worry that if spatial decisions are not controlled from the top, either directly or through sets of "impersonal" rules, then irresolvable conflicts that would drain the system and be an embarrassment to all will occur. Precise rules which tie physical facilities to positional level result partly from this need to have clear decision rules.

The other side of this view is seldom openly explored, namely, that the company is willing to trust its work tasks to its people, but not conflict-resolution tasks having to do with physical facilities. This confusing message will not enhance effectiveness. In addition, the organization gives up a potential resource, since spatial decisions can be used as a practice vehicle for *improving* conflict-resolution skills. Once again the visible, concrete nature of settings constitutes a good medium for this kind of learning, but also makes higher-level management feel that the organization cannot risk handling facilities issues in a participative manner.

Mobility

A very common reason given in organizations for allowing people to change their own work spaces is that they will not be in them very long, due to high positional mobility, and that changes would not be "fair" to the next occupant. This argument implies that alterations will be a greater affront or imposition than the decisions of some anonymous person in the hierarchy. My view is the opposite – that a place that has cumulative markings as a kind of history of its occupants is more human than a characterless box that is always being saved.

A good case can also be made for the proposition that if there is indeed a great deal of mobility within the system, then it is *more*, not less, important that people be able to alter a place quickly to reduce their settling-in time. A work force made up of people who feel transient hinders the development of a sense of community.[1]

Technical Blocks to Personal Influence

One reason for the difficulty of leaving personal markings is the characteristics of the materials and structures that are used in most organizations. As I noted earlier, Sheetrock, plaster walls, high-finish desks, etc., deteriorate with use rather than mellow and improve. There is a trend now toward the use of more rugged materials, such as the carpet-covered panels used in office landscaping. I hope that this trend continues. Features that can be changed easily give a person more influence over his own space. It is also worth reemphasizing that an older building is often considered to be more comfortable, partly because it has been lived in and also because an organization treats it differently. Since the building is already old, the organization is more likely to permit a broader range of uses and alterations. The building exists to be used by its occupants, not to be preserved as a monument. Similarly, rugged materials in a new building will not increase personal influence unless the system's rules allow alterations.

---

1 The mobility argument becomes even less valid when one begins to question the office-assignment system itself, which often requires a man to change offices with every status change. Physical transiency is reduced when this rigid rule is not applied.

Maintaining the Corporate Image

A great deal of the pressure for central control of facilities comes from executives who feel that the system must have the correct facilities to project the right image. This desire accounts for "integrated" interior designs which cannot be adjusted, because any variations would spoil the purity of the overall theme. There is indeed a difference between creating a setting that projects one sharp, clear image and developing facilities that mirror the more individualized choices of the people who constitute the system. In the "integrated theme" setting, I just wonder which executive it personally reflects and do not expect it to tell me very much about the real personality of the organization.

The desire for the correct image also accounts in part for the emphasis that is usually placed on keeping a work setting neat and clean. Because neatness is so important in our culture, many structural decisions reflect the desire to keep the facility clean and well-maintained rather than the purpose of the organization. Thus the real power of the maintenance department is to influence decisions about both new facilities and the rules which will govern the use of these facilities.

Power Relations

Obviously, a major cause of top-down spatial decisions is the power hierarchy in the organization. The simplest interpretation is that those in control use physical settings as a way of communicating the power structure by taking advantage of the symbolic language.

There is also a more subtle communication about power that contributes to the system's control over individuals' organizational life-spaces – the "doling-out" function of these decisions. Top management keeps control of facilities in order to have visible, tangible "things and stuff" to give out to "good" members at reward and promotion times. To relinquish facilities control would be to give up not only a symbolic communication medium, but also a set of carrots. The doling-out function is particularly strongly protected by top management in organizations where the nature of the tasks is not very intrinsically rewarding.

The concept of individual choice threatens the *stability* of the symbolic power language system in the organization. The fact that facilities are not just a budgetary problem becomes most obvious when a person proposes, for instance, to bring his own rug into his office. It is interesting to hear the arguments marshalled against his suggestion, especially if people are committed to avoiding direct mention of the status symbol process. I once suggested to an executive group that they try a new way of allocating resources by calculating what the company would budget for rugs and drapes (the status items) for a group, then giving the group that budget and letting them decide how to spend the money. My suggestion was met with silence, then with a rush of unconvincing reasons why it couldn't be done logistically. Finally, the subject was changed by one executive and was not brought up again until I mentioned the whole sequence in a feedback session on the group's process.

Blindness to the Impact of Settings

Many of the factors mentioned above would not have such an impact on spatial decisions if it were not for one important fact – in most organizations management is unaware of the potential connections between settings and the functioning of the organization. Since they see the provision of physical settings as simply another basic chore which is peripheral to the "real" tasks of the system, they lump physical facilities with other services, such as accounting and maintenance. The emphasis is thus put on doing what is most "efficient", i.e., least costly, rather than on what will be most useful for the workers' environment.

Over time, savings on facilities often become an end rather than a means to other ends. In tight budget periods this is particularly evident, as when a company saves a few thousand dollars by removing vital meeting spaces from their plans for a new building, thereby reducing both interaction and capacity to generate new ideas that could help them break their slump.

Inconspicuous Costs

The final factor, implied in the preceding discussion, is concerned with a general problem in human decision-making, that of accurately weighting the gains and costs of various alternatives. The concept that I have found most useful for understanding this process is *inconspicuous costs*. This term simply means that when an alternative involving a number of factors is being considered, some factors are less likely to be given a weight appropriate to their importance and are therefore the more "inconspicuous" costs (or gains).

For example, when a small group meets, the energy required for them to take a few minutes to decide what the setting should be like is more conspicuous than the possible costs of not doing so – costs such as inappropriate mood, too much psychological distance between the group members, and fatigue resulting from noise and bad lighting. Since taking action "costs more," the group often does not even consider what they have given up by *not* changing anything.

One of the most striking examples of the effect of inconspicuous costs is the process of buying a home. Consider two cases, Family A and Family B:

> Family A moved into a new city and bought a ranch-style tract house in a bland suburb. They did not really like the house or the neighborhood, but they felt that they had to protect themselves against the time four or five years hence when they would be moving and have to sell the house. Family B moved to the same city. They bought an old Victorian house with which they fell in love, in a central area that seemed very alive to them. They were warned by friends that the value of their house would not appreciate in that area and might even go down a bit.

In comparing the choices of the two families, we might conclude that each cared about different things. In fact, I think this is an unjustified conclusion and that it is more likely that B was better than A at recognizing the inconspicuous costs of buying according to the financial balance sheet. Family B recognized that there are many costs and gains connected with a family's home: the day-to-day contacts with people, the way the home structures their activities, the mood it creates and the extent to which it makes them want to be there, and many others. Family B was not willing to accept such costs for five years in order to satisfy only the criterion of not suffering a small economic loss on the house. Family A may well have bought five years of mediocre-to-bad living for their $2000-$5000 gain.

In this example the economic factor, because it can be measured, tends to drive out the life-style factors. In work organizations the same phenomenon occurs, and it is even more extreme because it is cumulative. The "services" orientation toward settings, plus the inconspicuous costs phenomenon, combine to focus most attention in organizational spatial decision-making on the initial installation and maintenance costs of the space. Much less attention is given to the less measurable costs to the organization's human resources or functioning. The capital outlays are conspicuous costs; the human system costs are fuzzy and inconspicuous.

As a consequence of these assumptions and forces, facilities planning tends to be delegated to accountants or office management people whose training and experience are almost exclusively in dealing with figures. It is therefore not surprising that the quantifiable costs – construction costs per square foot, cleaning costs per week – are weighted heavily and that the less quantifiable factors – decreases in stimulating contacts, lack of identification with the system – tend to be ignored when decisions are made. Numbers are easier to deal with, and they allow spatial decisions to be defended rationally (i.e., numerically). Thus, a circular process develops whereby blindness to the setting's impact leads top management to assign physical planning responsibility to "cost-cutters" (although management retains final decision authority) who then deal with the efficiency factors with which they are most familiar and comfortable – the costs of installation, cleaning, and change – thereby reinforcing top management's view that these are the important issues in facilities planning.

THE OTHER COSTS OF TOP-DOWN SPATIAL DECISIONS

I have singled out physical facilities control as an area where change is needed because I think the *human* costs of this pattern to the organization and its members are relatively high. I assume that a person's effectiveness and ability to take risks and responsibility for his actions increase as he is able to identify problems, make choices, take action, and get feedback about the consequences of his action. He becomes a greater resource to the system (and to himself) as he engages in this process.

The top-down decision process I have been describing *tends to stagnate and even reverse this pattern of growth*. Many people spend more waking time at work than in any other single activity. Their work setting, whether it is an office, a plant floor, a mill yard, or a ship's hold, is a major component of their psychological life space and is more concrete and visible than their place in the organization's social system. When a major piece of one's life space is controlled by someone else, a medium for problem-solving and testing one's own abilities is lost. The system sends the clear message to its members that they are not capable of being trusted with those kinds of decisions; hence, they get little practice and eventually come to believe that they are incapable of managing their own affairs.

This pattern is reinforced by similar control in other areas, such as career and promotional decisions. In the career area this may make some sense, since possibilities are dependent on so many organization-wide factors. But in work settings, top-down control only stifles growth and often leads to *poorer decisions* and inadequate settings on the task, social contact, security, and pleasure dimensions, since choices are being made by people who do not have the best information about the users' needs.

Another consequence of this process is that *people are trained to take little responsibility for the quality of their surroundings*. In essence they are taught that they do not "own" their surroundings; the company does, both economically and psychologically. This eventually leads to either poor settings or the organization's having to put a fairly large amount of effort into maintaining a setting. This effort would be unnecessary if the users felt responsible for their work places.[2] Of course, as I have discussed earlier, a boss may feel that these costs are a reasonable price to pay for his control of interaction, symbolic messages, and the like. My observations suggest, however, that he often opts for these gains without a very clear awareness of what he and others are losing on other dimensions.

For example, another long-term effect of top-down decisions about space is *the increased blindness of people to spatial influences*. Since they cannot change their settings anyway, people adapt by learning to shut off the frustration and other kinds of negative impact of their work settings. Although this reduces stress somewhat, it also leads to a self-perpetuating cycle whereby people unconsciously choose or accept settings which make their tasks more difficult. On numerous occasions I have watched a group meeting in a hotel or conference center enter the room and sit down wherever the chairs happened to be located. Thus, the group forms in the pattern that the hotel maintenance man thought was appropriate for a meeting. In some instances he may be right, but there is at least enough doubt to expect the group to take a moment to determine the most appropriate setting for its task. The fact that this is not done exemplifies pseudo-fixed space – people have been trained to be unaware of the difference that various arrangements can make.

Finally, all of these consequences – blocked growth, reduced sense of personal responsibility, and trained blindness to spatial influences – add

---

2 Manning (1965) observed that employees took much better care of washroom facilities in a new office building which they identified as "theirs"; Sommer (1969) notes that the daily litter in the Montreal subway system is measured in pounds, whereas in New York it is measured in tons. This is a good example of very different feelings about personal responsibility for one's setting.

Fig. 13.1 Soldiers at Fort Carson, Colorado, are now permitted to decorate their quarters to suit their own tastes. (Photograph by Carl Iwasaki. Reprinted from *Time*, December 21, 1970.)

up to *a reduction in a person's opportunities to experience his own humanity*. They lower his opportunity to be a feeling, thinking, problem-solving being who can be master of his own fate in dealing with his surroundings. It is no accident that when the United States Army began a drive to "humanize" its system, one of the first changes was to reduce the restrictions on what a man could do to his own quarters (see Fig. 13.1). The Army realized that the man's control over his environment was a necessary first step toward the high degree of self-control that would be expected of him in his future army life.

A FINAL DILEMMA

The conceptual differentiation of the six functions of settings was developed in large measure to deal with the kinds of costs and gains I have just discussed. My purpose has been to provide some dimensions that will help individuals and organizations take a more realistic and complex view of what they gain and lose when they choose certain physical structures over others. In this book I have not tried to provide hard and fast rules for the "best" way to lay out a plant or office, but rather to stimulate a *process* whereby consultants, users, and designers engage in a collaborative problem-solving process that is relevant to both the goals of the system *and* the human qualities of the people who will have to use the place. Whether or not this actually occurs will be an empirical question. One of the things most needed now is systematic research and evaluation of attempts to design facilities explicitly for organizational health.

There is an interesting process issue, however, which is likely to affect the degree to which organizations understand their own physical designs. One main theme here has been that the quality of an organization's setting influences the health of the system. Unfortunately, the converse also tends to be true – an organization that is "healthy"[3] will be more likely than an unhealthy one to make good decisions about its own space. The healthy organization will get more accurate information, process it better, understand more about the need for adaptability, and have a better sense of its identity and future. In other words *it is difficult to engage in a*

---

3 Although I will not go into detail about what constitutes a healthy organization, interested readers should read Bennis's (1966) propositions for defining criteria of organizational health.

healthy design process with an unhealthy system. The tendency is for an unhealthy system to choose settings which increase rather than reduce its problems.

On the other hand, the issue of space and restructuring settings is a common problem and as such is less threatening to a rigid organization than suggesting that the organizational processes and structure be systematically analyzed. I know of two recent instances where organizations started with space problems and gradually moved toward a wider examination of their needs for change when they encountered issues that could not be resolved on purely technical grounds. These systems were fortunate enough to have a team of space consultants that was aware of the organizational issues involved. A more traditional design firm would have reinforced a defensive management's tendency to define the issues as merely problems of technical design or cost efficiency.

In a sense this brings us full circle. The proposition on which this book was based is that organizational development specialists need to consider the physical system as well as the social system, so that the clients' physical systems support their change efforts. Designers must also consider the more hidden aspect of their traditional task and pay more attention to the social system change processes required to develop and execute a really good physical design for the client system.

In other words, I feel that the possibilities have not been fully realized. Behavioral scientists should seek the help of designers, and designers should seek the help of applied behavioral scientists when working with a complex client system. But most important, both of these professional groups must be sure to include the vital third member of the team – the client. It is easy to forget this step in the excitement of applying one's specialty to a new area.

The typical client organization has usually resisted or ignored the possibilities of including behavioral scientists in the process of physically structuring the system, mainly for the reasons discussed above, and also because of the tendency to organize problems into categories like "organization," "facilities," and so on.

The *process* by which physical settings are structured is, in many cases, a more powerful influence on employees than is the actual shape of the structure. A setting which is a constant reminder of its users' lack of control over their own life space will be a powerful block to the development of more humanistic work organizations, and it will also usually be less appropriate and satisfactory for the real needs of the users.

To avoid these costs, office design and organization development processes must include in their definition of clients the users of the place as active collaborators with the professional change agents.

This process of collaboration will not go smoothly at first. The characteristics I discussed above – taking little responsibility, unawareness of the costs of bad settings, and feeling that people are less competent than they really are – have been consistently drummed into employees, and there is no reason to expect an immediate change in attitude. But this does not justify top management's (convenient) view that people cannot take responsibility for their own settings. It instead defines a problem in the process of change, and I believe this is where consultants can have a great impact. It should be a consultant's goal to work with designers to both overcome top management's resistance to change (through evidence of net benefits), and to design training experiences which will help lower-level employees develop their competence and ability to influence their immediate surroundings in the organization.

REFERENCES

Allen, T. "Meeting the technical information needs of research and development projects," MIT Industrial Liaison Program Report, no. 13-314, November, 1969.

Altman, I. and W. Haythorn. "The ecology of isolated groups," *Behavl. Sci.*, 12, 3, 1967.

Ardrey, R. *The Territorial Imperative*. New York: Atheneum, 1966.

Barker, R. *Ecological Psychology*. Stanford, Calif.: Stanford University Press, 1968.

Blauner, R. *Alienation and Freedom*. Chicago: University of Chicago Press, 1964.

Buckley, W. "A soulless administration?" *Boston Globe*, Dec. 14, 1970, p. 7.

"Bürolandschaft," *Progressive Architecture*, May 1968.

Caplan, A. and J. Lindsay. "An experimental investigation of the effects of high temperature on the efficiency of workers in deep mines," *Bull. Instn. Min. Metall.*, 480,1948.

Carr, S. and K. Lynch. "Where learning happens," *Daedalus*, 97, 4, 1968.

"Chaos as a system," *Progressive Architecture*, January 1969.

Duhl, L. "Planning is politics: a case study of a community conflict," *Ekistics*, 26, 155, October 1968.

Ellis, W. "Lebanon: little bible land in the crossfire of history," *National Geographic*, 137, 2, Feb. 1970.

"First design award," *Progressive Architecture*, January 1970.

Festinger, L., S. Schachter, and K. Back. *Social Pressures in Informal Groups: a study of human factors in housing*. New York: Harper & Row, 1950.

Fiske, D. "Effects of monotonous and restricted stimulation," in Fiske and Maddi, 1961, pp. 106-144.

Fiske, D. and S. Maddi. *Functions of Varied Experience*. Homewood, Ill.: Dorsey Press, 1961.

Goffman, E. *Behavior in Public Places*. Glencoe, Ill.: The Free Press, 1963.

Goffman, E. *The Presentation of Self in Everyday Life*. Garden City, N.Y.: Doubleday Anchor, 1959.

Hall, E. "The language of space," *Landscape*, Fall 1960.

Hall, E. *The Hidden Dimension*. Garden City, N.Y.: Doubleday, 1966.

Hearn, G. "Leadership and the spatial factor in small groups," *J. of abnorm. soc. Psychol.*, 54, 1957.

Homans, G. *The Human Group*. New York: Harcourt Brace & World, 1950.

"Jumbo beats the gremlins," *Time*, July 13, 1970.

Katz, E. and P. Lazarsfeld. *Personal Influence*. Glencoe, Illinois: The Free Press 1955.

Kleinschrod, W. "The case for office landscape," *Administrative Management*, October, 1966.

Kohl, H. *The Open Classroom*. New York: New York Review (Vintage), 1969.

Kurtz, S. "From grid to growth," *Progressive Architecture*, Nov., 1969.

Leavitt, H. "Some effects of certain communication patterns on group performance," *J. abnorm. soc. Psychol.*: 46, 1951.

Lynch, K. and M. Rivkin. "A walk around the block," *Landscape*, 8, 1969 (reprinted in Proshansky *et al.*, 1970).

Manning, P. *Office Design: A Study of Environment*. Liverpool, England: The Pilkington Research Unit, 1965. (Reprinted in part in Proshansky, *et al.*, 1970.)

Maslow, A. *Motivation and Personality*. New York: Harper & Brothers, 1954.

Maslow A. and N. Mintz. "Effects of aesthetic surroundings," *J. Psychol.*, 41, 1956.

McClelland, D. *The Achieving Society*. New York: Van Nostrand, 1961.

McGregor, D. *The Human Side of Enterprise*. New York: McGraw-Hill 1960.

Michelson, W. "Analytic sampling for design information: a survey of housing experience," *Proceedings of First Conference of the Environmental Design Research Association,* Chapel Hill, June 1969 (H. Sanoff, ed.).

Mogulescu, M. *Profit Through Design*. New York: American Management Association, 1970.

Neustadt, R. *Presidential Power*. New York: John Wiley, 1960.

"New British prison has pin-up facilities," *The New York Times*, Jan. 3, 1971, p. 9.

"Offices of the year," *Administrative Management*, 31, 3, March 1970.

Orwell, G. *Down and out in Paris and London*. New York: Harcourt Brace & World 1933 (Berkeley Medallion paperback edition, 1959).

Orwell, G. *The Road to Wigan Pier*. New York: Harcourt Brace & World, 1937 (Berkeley Medallion paperback edition, 1961).

Osmond, H. "Some psychiatric aspects of design," in Holland, L. (Ed.) *Who Designs America*?, New York: Anchor, 1966.

Parkinson, C. *Parkinson's Law and Other Studies in Administration*. London: Penguin, 1959.

Parr, A. "Design for eye and mind," *Industrial Design*, 16, 7, 1969.

Parr, A. "Psychological aspects of urbanology," *J. Social Issues*, 22, 4, 1966.

Perls, F., R. Hefferline, and P. Goodman. *Gestalt Therapy*. New York: Julian Press (also Delta Paperback) 1951.

Platt, J. "Beauty: pattern and change," in D. Fiske and S. Maddi, *Functions of Varied Experience.* Homewood, Ill.: Dorsey Press, 1961, pp. 402-430.

Poulton, E., N. Hitchings and R. Brooker. "Effect of cold and rain upon the vigilance of lookouts," *Ergonomics*, 8, 1965.

Proshansky, H., W. Ittelson and J. Rivlin. *Environmental Psychology*. New York: Holt, Rinehart and Winston, 1970.

Raven, J. "Sociological evidence on housing 2: the home environment," *The Architectural Review*, September 1967.

Roethlisberger, F. and W. Dickson. *Management and the Worker*. Cambridge: Harvard University Press, 1939.

Rotter, J. "Generalised expectancies for internal versus external control of reinforcement," *Psychology Monogr.*, 80, 1, whole no, 609, 1966.

Schachtel, E. "On memory and childhood amnesia," in *Metamorphosis*, New York: Basic Books, 1959.

Schein, E. *Process Consultation*. Reading, Mass.: Addison-Wesley, 1969.

Schroder, H., M. Driver and S. Streufert. *Human Information Processing*. New York: Holt, Rinehart & Winston 1967.

Schutz, W. *Joy*. New York: Grove Press, 1968.

Smith, C.R. "The great museum debate," *Progressive Architecture*, December 1969.

Sommer, R. "Classroom ecology," *J. App. Beh. Sci.*, 3, 4, 1967a.

Sommer, R. "Small group ecology," *Psychol. Bull.*, 67, 2, 1967b.

Sommer, R. *Personal Space: The Behavioral Basis of Design*. Englewood Cliffs, N.J.: Prentice-Hall (Spectrum) 1969.

Sonnenfeld, J. "Variable values in space and landscape: an inquiry into the nature of environmental necessity," *J. of Social Issues*, 22, 4, 1966.

Speer, A. *Inside the Third Reich*. New York: Macmillan, 1970.

"Stairway to success," *Newsweek*, October 24, 1966, p. 99.

Steele, F. "The impact of the physical setting on the social climate at two comparable laboratory sessions," *Human Relations Training News*, 12, 4, 1968.

Steele, F. "Organization development and sticks and stones," *Office Deisgn*, 7, 5, 1969.

Steele, F. "Physical settings and organization development," in H. Hornstein, W. Burke, B. Benedict, R. Lewicki, and M. Hornstein (Eds.), *Strategies of Social Change: A Behavioral Science Analysis*, Glencoe, Ill.: The Free Press, 1971.

Steinzor, B. "The spatial factor in face-to-face discussion groups," *J. abnorm. soc. Psychol.*, 45, 1950.

Trist, E. and K. Bamforth. "Some social and psychological consequences of the longwall method of coal-getting," *Human Relations*, 4, 1951.

Wade, J. "Disposal," *Industrial Design,* June 1968.

Waugh, E. *Decline and Fall*. 1928 (Penguin edition, 1937).

White, R. "Motivation reconsidered: the concept of competence," *Psychol. Rev.*, 66, 1959.

Zinsser, W. "As jumbo jets arrive and liners depart, must shuffleboard roll on forever?" *Life*, Jan. 23, 1970.